Praise for *Reconstructing Inclusion*

"Amri Johnson has gifted us with a worthy exploration of the current state of DEI work, and more importantly has challenged our thinking with this substantive and thoughtful work. At a time when tribalism is splintering societies around the world, and when divisiveness exists even within political and social ideologies, Johnson brings a mindset of 'both/and' to a field that is mired in 'either/or' thinking. As a native-born American with significant experiences in Europe and South America, he broadens our understanding of what is needed to bring people into alignment on a global scale. He recognizes the need for individual awareness, collective action, and structural change, and as an accomplished professional who has worked both inside and outside of organizations, he shows us tangible ways to get there. This book is a powerful resource for anybody who is looking at forging pathways to inclusion and belonging."

—**Howard Ross, author,**
Everyday Bias **and** *Our Search for Belonging*

"*Reconstructing Inclusion* is an invaluable input for leaders who want to go beyond normative approaches to DEI and people issues in organizations, and create substantive and sustainable change. Particularly on-point is Johnson's warning about giving primacy to single dimensions of identity. In a polarized society ridden with a focus on human sub-groups and the divisions between them, this book centres humanity as a whole without losing sight of the need to address racial and other forms of social injustice. If DEI is to really enable progress, this balanced approach seems like the only viable way. There has perhaps never been a more important time for a book such as this, and I highly recommend it. Readers (and their organizations) will benefit from the wisdom it contains."

—**Sukhvinder S. Obhi, Professor of Social
Neuroscience, McMaster University, Canada**

"It's hard to keep up with the abundance of books being published on DEI. But don't miss this one. Amri Johnson writes as a friendly critic inside the DEI movement. He beautifully weaves together his story as a Black man with his experience inside a massive pharmaceutical company and shares rich insights about what needs to change in DEI. This groundbreaking book brings cultural intelligence to life."

—**David Livermore, author and leading authority
on cultural intelligence**

"Amri Johnson offers a call for practitioners to break the cycle of waxing and waning and not advancing DEI in the ways we desire. This means being in community to co-create our DEI vision, and being dedicated to changing our methods and patterns of behavior. This book offers the opportunity to think differently, to scrutinize methods and be open to 'unlearn' what has been steeped into our practices and relearn, as a continuous process, concepts such as, 'othering, meritocracy, intersectionality, and exclusion.' I highly recommend this book especially for DEI practitioners who want to be included and inclusive in affecting accessible, actionable, and sustainable organizations through diversity, equity, and inclusion."

—**Carla Carten, PhD, MSOD, Interim Senior Vice President and Chief Diversity, Equity, and Inclusion Officer, Mass General Brigham**

"Any leader who is committed to fostering a culture of inclusion needs to read this insightful and paradigm-shifting book. As strategic as he is pragmatic, Amri Johnson takes us on a critical journey that will leave any leader rethinking how to sustainably make manifest true inclusion at work."

—**Susan MacKenty Brady, Deloitte Ellen Gabriel Chair for Women in Leadership and Founding CEO, Simmons University Institute for Inclusive Leadership**

"*Reconstructing Inclusion* took me on a journey of exploration and learning. It allowed me to be curious about my personal views about DEI whilst allowing other views to be listened to and explored. The non-binary approach taken brings layers of the subject into view and allows one to peel them away one by one and then put them back together again. Whilst the book is not a tool kit, it has reminded me how intent actions and systemic inclusion are paramount. Creating inclusion as a state of being is not the responsibility of 'them.' We are all guardians of inclusion."

—**Petra Battersby, FCIPD, Chief People Officer, Envision Pharma Group**

"*Reconstructing Inclusion* is a strong message for global organizations who are interested in truly advancing Diversity, Equity and Inclusion in a meaningful way. Amri Johnson's assertion is that deconstructing inclusion allows for expanding structures beyond reducing terms as simply effective vs. ineffective. Instead, addressing the complexity organizations should face to really move the needle. His book clearly amplifies what needs to be done to ensure measurable outcomes and success."

—**Michael Hyter, President and CEO, The Executive Leadership Council (ELC)**

Reconstructing
Inclusion

Reconstructing Inclusion

Making DEI Accessible, Actionable, and Sustainable

AMRI B. JOHNSON

Matt Holt Books
An Imprint of BenBella Books, Inc.
Dallas, TX

Matt Holt is an imprint of BenBella Books, Inc.
10440 N. Central Expressway
Suite 800
Dallas, TX 75231
benbellabooks.com
Send feedback to feedback@benbellabooks.com

BenBella and *Matt Holt* are federally registered trademarks.

Printed in the United States of America
10 9 8 7 6 5 4 3 2 1

Library of Congress Control Number: 2022013470
ISBN 9781637741887 (hardcover)
ISBN 9781637741894 (digital)

Editing by Gregory Newton Brown
Copyediting by Michael Fedison
Proofreading by Isabelle Rubio and Ariel Fagiola
Indexing by WordCo
Text design and composition by PerfecType, Nashville, TN
Cover design by Sold Brands Ltd
Printed by Lake Book Manufacturing

For my father, Larry D. Johnson, Sr. (1940-2017).
Your integrity, wisdom, and compassion are an
eternal flame in my heart and mind.

Contents

Introduction

"But we are all androgynous, not only because we are all born of
a woman impregnated by the seed of a man but because each of
us, helplessly and forever, contains the other—male in female,
female in male, white in Black and Black in white. We are a part
of each other. Many of my countrymen appear to find this fact
exceedingly inconvenient and even unfair, and so, very often, do
I. But none of us can do anything about it."

—**"Here Be Dragons," James Baldwin, 1985**

The notion of "belonging" has been among the more popular concepts
of modern diversity, equity, and inclusion (DEI) practice. Most of my
colleagues view it in the Maslowian sense of the term.[1] The psychologist's "Hierarchy of Needs" theory articulates that once our essential phys-
iological needs (i.e., water, food, shelter, sleep) and our safety and security
needs (i.e., sense of safety from external threat, financial well-being) are met,
humans need a sense of belongingness—the sense of intimacy, trust, giving
and receiving affection, community, or being part of something greater than
oneself. Current DEI thought sees the fulfillment of this need as "the key"
to unlocking inclusion.

1

The idea of belonging isn't restricted to an individual's sense. In fact, it's not at all oriented toward the "I" or "me" that's often purported in psychology circles and the world of DEI. In the Blackfoot (Siksika) Nation (by whom scholars say Maslow's philosophy was strongly influenced[2]), belonging is a collective notion—a communal "we" that leads community and self purposefully toward actualization.

An increasing number of DEI professionals have added the word "belonging" to their titles or department names. They often do so with monikers such as Director, Office of Inclusion and Belonging; Vice President of Diversity, Inclusion, Belonging, and Equity; and Chief Inclusion, Belonging, and Diversity Officer. These title changes are considered an evolution of the purpose of traditional offices of Diversity and Inclusion or Inclusion and Diversity.

These changes in terminology often seem to me like fool's gold. They are shiny. They look great when we're preaching about "the work." Yet I feel we often miss the mark of determining how we "get there." Why aren't we there already? And where is "there"? Most organizations haven't even arrived at what they initially sought out to do. So why add another thing to solve for?

When I entered the DEI field, things seemed straightforward. I entered as a public health professional, an epidemiologist committed to health equity. From this lens, the scientific data, particularly around mortality and morbidity, were indisputable. Causes were being found, and other questions were emerging about social determinants of health. Any reasonable person looking at the statistics could say without argument that differences in health outcomes between rich and poor, and whites and most minorities, even after controlling for social-economic status, were real.

Upon moving deeper into what I call "corporate DEI" (to distinguish from my public health view), my perspective was broadened. As an entrepreneur, I saw the profitability potential of the DEI field. In 2002, when I started my job board platform, Diversity HealthWorks, we can estimate that $1 to $2 billion was spent annually in the industry. Companies were spending about $8 billion on diversity efforts in 2017, according to the consulting firm McKinsey & Company. Not bad.

As I learned the field's contemporary lexicon, I realized that people don't want to be "tolerated." It's not cool (anymore) to "manage diversity" because "diverse" people don't want to be managed; they want to be led and to lead themselves. More importantly, they want to be included. Thus, we have increasingly put a greater weight on "inclusion."

This focus didn't last long. Practitioners, including myself, started turning toward unconscious bias and the reality that we all have it. Unconscious bias was immediately well received and has become a normalized part of the diversity, equity, and inclusion lexicon over the past two decades. Ample resources are put into unconscious bias training and developing tools to mitigate bias in everything from job descriptions, hiring, succession planning, team selection, and meetings. Awareness has increased, and for some organizations, this greater awareness has led to structural and systems changes to mitigate bias. For others, the educational efforts haven't translated into tangible outcomes (increased representation, the perception of less discrimination, lowered micro-aggressions, etc.). So the conclusion (wrongly and prematurely arrived at in my opinion) has been that unconscious bias training doesn't work.

Thus, belonging is a newer hot topic. Couple that with movements such as #MeToo and #BlackLivesMatter and the focus has narrowed to single identity–focused belongingness. What if our shift was cyclical and perhaps premature? What if we need to be focused on really getting our minds, arms, and hearts around the complexities of humanity, rather than reducing ourselves to memes, movements, and hashtags?

More American

During my time working for a Swiss-based pharmaceutical company's research division in Cambridge, Massachusetts, I was introduced to Europe in a more up-close manner. Traveling to Switzerland and other European countries multiple times a year, I learned a few things about life there. I take more coffee breaks and show-and-tell meetings now. I know what an "apero" (after work hours) is and attend them regularly. I use my fork and knife regardless of what I'm eating (sans cereal and dessert). And I generally feel my family is safe all the time when they are out of the house (at least in Switzerland, Spain, the UK, France, and Germany, where I have spent the most time). Maslow would approve.

When I first started working for the pharmaceutical company, I never considered living in Europe. I'd spent a good amount of time working to build business in Brazil, and I thought long and hard about living in Brazil. But in Europe? No. This was mainly because of my lack of context, or because my context was that all of the European countries I might consider living in were colonizers—the Netherlands, Belgium, France, Portugal, England, and Spain. Yet, I was born into a country that was colonized and grew to be a colonizer itself, doing so with tactics as brutal as those historically enacted by European nations. The idea of colonization wasn't at the top of mind, but it sat in my subconscious, emerging periodically.

In 2019, after spending more than forty-eight years of life living and working in the United States, I started a new journey. I now live primarily outside of the US. Of course, my identity is plural, but as I've moved through the world, central to who I've considered myself to be has been my identity as a Black man, Black brother, Black son, Black leader, Black epidemiologist, Black thinker. These constructs are choices, and ones that I would make again given the same circumstances, even with the insight I've gained about my Blackness through living abroad.

When I spent time in Brazil, I recognized that I was a "gringo" and that most locals in my neighborhood thought of me as "O Americano" (the American). Nonetheless, seeing the dynamics of social economics and hearing stories of the struggles of darker-skinned Brazilians to elevate, I felt as Black as always.

I might now describe myself a bit differently: as born into a Christian spiritualist family, native of Topeka, Kansas; height 6'3" (192cm), weight 235 pounds (107kg), vegetarian, Republican-raised, married to a Spanish woman (whose primary language is French), and lives in Switzerland— who happens to be Black. In fact, the longer I live in Europe, the less my

Blackness is on my mind. For the first time in my life, I feel more American than Black.

My politics and ethics are principle-based. I don't lean heavily to the Left or the Right. With extremes, I am cautious. In yin and yang theory, when one aspect goes to an extreme, it will begin to reverse in the opposite direction. The world of DEI has reached peaks in terms of advocacy. The backlash to that advocacy, whether it be over the representation of women and minorities, transgender rights, or an idea like intersectionality, has unleashed a vitriolic set of behaviors that many—particularly those in the so-called *developed world*[3]—thought had been eradicated.

My Americanness has been so pervasive that I find myself having nostalgic sentiments for things I mostly took for granted when still in my native land. Interestingly, one of the sentiments that stands out is from the movie *The Wizard of Oz*, based on the book series by L. Frank Baum. The line spoken by Dorothy to her on-screen cairn terrier has come into my consciousness more frequently than I want to admit: "Toto, we're not in Kansas anymore."

I've never read L. Frank Baum's books, including *The Wonderful Wizard of Oz* (though I may do so now). Most people simply watched the 1939 movie. Some have never seen the original movie, or mostly remember a 1978 version, *The Wiz*, which was directed by Sidney Lumet with musical direction by the prolific Quincy Jones. *The Wiz* was a Black film (except for the director). It's a classic among Black Americans as it featured Motown greats Diana Ross and Michael Jackson. It was indeed the first time Jackson and Jones came together musically. Their relationship following *The Wiz* is legendary.[4]

What stands out to me in both film adaptations is the music, the symbolism, and their relatability. The characters—a Tin Man looking for a heart, a Lion searching for courage, and a Scarecrow yearning for a brain, all led by Dorothy, who was simply trying to return home—had qualities that made them approachable and elevated their vulnerability and relatability. Furthermore, the metaphors of overcoming self-doubt and acting on behalf of others despite one's self-perceived fears are universally inspirational.

And then there's the music. Harold Arlen and Yip Harburg composed "Over the Rainbow," the 1939 movie's signature song, sung by Judy Garland. After singing the song publicly for many years, Garland said, "The song has become a part of my life. It is symbolic of everybody's dream and that's why people get tears in their eyes when they hear it. I have sung it dozens of times and it's still the song that is closest to my heart."[5] The song was deemed *the* American song of the twentieth century. Many different versions have been made since. My favorite is Hawaiian singer Israel "Iz" Kamakawiwo'ole's ukulele version, which posthumously climbed the international charts in 2004.

With the arrival of our son Kai, who was born in Switzerland in 2019, we were gifted many stuffed animals that played music. About half of them played the melody to "Over the Rainbow." I found this comforting. The gifts were purchased in central Europe, and I discovered that while many people, including my wife, were familiar with the tune, few of them had seen the film or knew the song originated from the film.

Imagine how American I felt explaining the context to them. I've yet to get my wife to sit down and watch the film. It may end up being a few years until my son can comprehend it.

Why Even Deal with This Quirky Field?

The Wizard of Oz and *The Wiz* are among my favorite movie classics. They qualify for that small bucket of films that I can watch repeatedly and still enjoy. Interestingly, L. Frank Baum was a women's suffrage supporter. He contributed financially and undauntedly to that cause, serving for some time as secretary to his local women's suffrage club. Conversely, some of his writings can be interpreted as having racist undertones toward Native Americans and Black Americans. I don't share this interpretation. Still, criticism of some of his essays reached a point that Baum's family issued a public apology for any harm his writing had brought the Sioux tribe.[6]

This knowledge might trigger many DEI practitioners to dismiss Baum and his entire canon. He'd be labeled as "anti" this or that, or as a racist (not an "anti-racist"). This expected response would be considered acceptable despite Baum's commitment to women and the inspiration of his work.

Responses of this kind do very little good for inclusion's evolution in organizational life. I would go as far as to say that advocating aggressively for a single identity, particularly the one a person identifies with most strongly, is part of the reason that most diversity work is at best "ceremonial." It will continue to be so if those in practice make their activism primarily about their personal interests or if the intent is to get something from someone or for someone.

My question is, what are we trying to get? If representation increases, what do we do next? If we focus on retention and the numbers stay the same, what do we do next? If the numbers go up, what do we do next? If our organizational climate/engagement survey data say, "we are an inclusive organization now," what do we do next?

Much of the work I've seen during the past twenty years has been meaningful to some and less so to others. Neither right nor wrong, this work has mostly lacked the momentum to shift organizational gravity toward inclusion as a fundamental element in business success. By continuing to repeat these incomplete efforts, we may be holding back a part of the puzzle that we need to get diversity and inclusion unstuck. We must continue doing the work, without doubt. However, first we must think differently about how we do our work, including advocating for greater representation and retention. We need to consider whether what we're doing serves the entire organization in an accessible, actionable, and sustainable manner.

Many times over the past several years I've been ready to abandon DEI as a profession. I have questioned what I have done and what I am doing. I wondered if this path was nothing more than a egoistic waste of resources that wouldn't result in anything of significance.

Conversely, I have watched many practitioners sincerely give their all to this work while experiencing equal or greater frustration. The desire to see change is real and soul stirring. I see organizations that place inclusion in their mission, consider it a core piece of their aspirational culture, and are doing all they can based on what has been set out—usually by consulting firms—as "best practice."

More than fifty years after the beginning of diversity practices, the primary shifts that we're aiming for haven't been realized. Thus, my reason for doing this work has shifted.

I continue to do this work because:

- I am convicted that choosing humanity and doing so consistently is the co-creation of everyone (inside and outside of organizations).

- I am clear there is no "them." Our efforts to elevate our organizations must be connected to elevating the societies in which we reside. The thought of a "them" in contemporary business is erroneous. There is no way that a similar-minded "us" will know all that's needed to be known to grow a business with all its complexities and perpetual changes.

- I have a vision of the world my children will inherit. A world where most citizens around the globe recognize our inseparable interdependence. My vision sees organizational leaders who are compelled to design their firms with inclusivity as an essential structural element toward sustainable success.

- I believe that future generations will depend on collaboration more than competition and that the most successful businesses will be purpose-driven and inherently collaborative. Moreover, those building such businesses will do so with integrity and caring that benefits the greater good without compromise.

- I have been given so much grace, and I can certainly never repay it to all in the universe who have bestowed it upon me. This work, and this book, is my small attempt at doing so.

- I know that this is core to my life's work. It is independent of the organization I work for and the role I play for that organization. It is about Being—I hope that the doing will reflect that.

There is no "key" to this massive puzzle of diversity, equity, and inclusion in organizations. In fact, there are multiple puzzles, and they require different tools to solve them. My intention is not to present another tool kit. This is not a how-to book. My aim is to foster a co-created framework. One that fosters dialogue, opens hearts, and inspires possibility to create the extraordinary.

Part
One

Part
One

What Is Reconstructing Inclusion?

"Out of the crooked timber of humanity, no straight thing was ever made."

—**Immanuel Kant (1724–1804)**

The idea of diversity has never been more present in the minds of people throughout world history. Organizations and institutions have come to recognize that pluralism, despite resistance to certain concepts by a vocal minority, isn't optional in contemporary workspaces, whether digital or analog. Diversity is inevitable, and demographic destiny is increasingly manifesting itself.

While companies' increased efforts to include the visible and less visible differences in their organizations aren't new, most are placing an intensive focus on inclusion (along with equity) due to highly publicized incidents of inhumane treatment of historically marginalized groups.

The murder of George Floyd in Minneapolis in 2020 was recorded and broadcast over social media. Other video footage, such as the ambush of

Ahmaud Arbery in Brunswick, Georgia, brought global attention to the underlying motivation of those committing these crimes.

Racist acts are not new. They didn't start in 2017 with the inauguration of a United States president who many perceived as racist. Inequitable, violent, and discriminatory acts have plagued organizations across the planet since recorded history. So, why the increased attention now?

We could make many hypotheses. In my work deconstructing the history of diversity and inclusion programs, I have found that many programs most of us have acknowledged as best practices have produced slim results where equity in companies or society is concerned. The work of leading researchers in analyzing these efforts primarily shows they have failed. Many interventions weren't structured to succeed.

Recruitment and training have been particularly sad. In recruitment, organizations have set goals for increasing representation by sex, race, and other protected classes. Some of the world's biggest tech companies, such as Google and Meta (formerly Facebook), have people responsible for sourcing candidates from underrepresented backgrounds. While results have been relatively small and incremental, Meta's *efforts* can be applauded. Fifty-three percent of Meta's technical staff are of Asian heritage, a 12 percent increase from 2014. Blacks and Hispanics make up a total of 6 percent of technical roles. Yet only 25.4 percent of the company's leadership—a 6 percent increase since 2014—is Asian. Blacks and Hispanics represent 8 percent. Similar numbers can be found at Google.

Does this mean Asians are technically adept, but not so much where leadership is concerned? Probably not. The "why" for how Asians are less represented in leadership than they are in technical roles has not been publicly explored by either firm. What does this mean for other groups whose growth in leadership and technical roles has been even less substantial? What if Meta or Google had only grown their revenue by 12 percent between 2014 and 2020? Would their stakeholders be satisfied with that growth? The answer is a definite "no."

Picking on big tech is easy given its brand ubiquity and relatively trans-parent representation data. The reality: they're not the only companies ineq-uitably hiring in Silicon Valley, or elsewhere around the world. Thousands of firms have invested in education and training interventions intended to bolster their DEI efforts. Most of them have seen similar outcomes in terms of recruitment and retention of employees from underrepresented groups.

When I joined my former employer, the research division of Novartis, we led with inclusion instead of representation. We looked at our approach as one of systemic and cultural change from the outset. Did we have gaps related to representation still? Yes.

We recognized that to increase representation, we needed to create the behavioral and structural conditions for long-term sustainability. We could have gone to the HR organization and compelled them to change hiring policies. Instead, we began by creating behavioral expectations with lead-ership teams, scientific collaborations with scientists and institutions from parts of the world that were historically not highly considered (e.g., vari-ous African countries and South America), and traineeships that brought in young scholars who generally had exposure disparities but were highly motivated and as capable as students coming from branded schools. We did things like unconscious bias education. And we followed that up with action steps and behavioral inputs that came to be normative for most leaders and their groups. Subsequently, representation also modestly increased. What we implemented based on evidence, along with building approaches with and eventually driven by employees, thrived.

Organizations are interested in diversity, equity, and inclusion like never before. Heightened media attention, political shifts, generational acceptance, and academic research have made clear to many people who have previously ignored DEI that toxicity in workplace culture is threatening productivity, recruitment, employee retention, health, and well-being.

Companies are falling over themselves as they rush to invest in and hire DEI consultants and whatever else is needed to give their workplaces a good grade on these issues. We are witnessing unprecedented investments in unconscious bias training, diversity recruitment, and, more recently, anti-racism education. If most of these approaches have had a questionable impact in the past, what makes us think they will create instrumental change today?

Considering these past results, what should we do differently to make diversity, inclusion, equity, and their related efforts instrumental in organizational advancement and fulfillment of purpose?

My answer: *purposeful deconstruction.*

When I talk about deconstruction, I am talking about a cool-headed analysis of whether these fundamental concepts that many DEI practitioners use actually work.

Deconstructing Inclusion

One could argue that a considerable amount of deconstruction—the sociopolitical and economic kind—has taken place over many years and has accelerated via the many intersecting conditions of a global pandemic. The novel coronavirus has uncovered how we have failed to engage with tensions in a way that recognizes them as steps toward maintaining a functioning society.

The stark differences in how companies and nation-states engaged with their people around COVID-19 revealed polarities and levels of complexity that weren't new. However, the impetus for addressing them before our economies and all the formal and informal structures that maintain them came to an abrupt shutdown, for many, was about trying to get "problems" resolved as quickly as possible. It's like being irritated by the sound of a squeaky wheel and deciding to spray oil on it. For other complex issues like climate change, racial justice, dynamics of remote work, poverty, and disparities in higher education, we have focused on them periodically, imagining that we will eventually bring solutions to the table for each.

The pandemic has acted like a giant microscope that amplified and magnified complex social issues. Unlike previous local tragedies (hurricanes, earthquakes, and other epidemics), this one went global. Everyone on the planet has been impacted. Whether a country has had one case (like the Federated States of Micronesia) or eighty million plus (like the United States), the nature of the disease and its effect has shown our global and local interdependencies in ways that none of us could have predicted.

Societal tension is reality. Most democracies were formed through tensions and have evolved as a result. Even in societies where democracy is not the prevailing system, tensions are central to growing societies. They play a critical role in how decisions that impact citizens or subjects are made and enacted. From this, we can conclude that tension exists in any system where difference exists. It's inevitable, and if one considers its function (think— what forces keep a bridge from collapsing?), then even when it is not comfortable, we can at least know that it is necessary.

When purposeful deconstruction is done, tensions, contradictions, and paradoxes serve as springboards as we adapt to the complexities behind them.

The idea of deconstruction is not new. It was created and has been profoundly influenced by French philosopher Jacques Derrida, who coined the term "deconstruction." Derrida argues that in Western culture, people tend to think and express their thoughts in terms of binary oppositions (white and black, masculine and feminine, cause and effect, conscious and unconscious, presence and absence, speech and writing). Derrida believed that these oppositions are socially constructed hierarchies with one term that a predominant culture views as positive or superior and another that is considered negative or subordinate. To deconstruct such binaries to cast a spotlight on perceived hierarchy is at the heart of Derrida's philosophy.

In the first part of the book, I will non-exhaustively deconstruct the language that DEI practitioners use to make sense of what organizations and institutions seek to create for their people and cultures. When I use the term "practitioner," I refer to anyone who has become familiar with and regularly uses the terms I will discuss. I intend to create space, welcoming more people to enter the conversation and become practitioners by making the language used by DEI professionals less exclusive.

The journey into deconstructing DEI has, in a way, already begun through the sociopolitical and economic deconstruction that we have seen increasingly since early 2020. Over time, we have modified our approaches from diversity management to cultural competency; a more deliberate focus on inclusion, belonging, and equity, and more recently, a revisiting of social justice through anti-racism and racial equity. The list goes on.

Organizations and those who have been passionate about "the work" (a phrase often used by DEI practitioners) have changed their terminology based on their objectives, past negative connotations, and misinterpretations. In some cases, those responsible for naming their departments and offices are working to create a brand that sounds more appealing and less tied to the approaches perceived as correlated with failure to increase the representation of underrepresented, underexposed, and in some cases excluded identities across a broad range of industries and their respective institutions.

Deconstructing inclusion does not mean annihilation. To the contrary, it is an expansion beyond the structures that have often reduced certain terms and practices to effective versus ineffective, and in some cases have rendered such approaches as no longer viable in place of the preferred approach of a popular individual or ideological group. The problem with this sort of reductionism is that there is great complexity in organizations. To think that any single approach or mindset that holds potential benefit for one firm holds equal benefit for all is a gross assumption, and incomplete at best.

With purposeful deconstruction I examine historical diversity and inclusion concepts to provide context. They are broken down to examine how they serve the field, practitioners, and the organizations they work for around the world. This part of the book also provides a critical and accessible view of the concepts to make them more useful to organizations.

Beyond criticizing things like training, the field has been stunted. Experienced practitioners' lack of incisive exploration and challenge to the current paradigm has weakened DEI's transformative potential. At best, the outcomes lead to inconsistent understanding in the organizational implementation of DEI programs. At worst, it leaves some people in organizations (often quite influential ones) with the sense that "the work" is for someone else.

Thus, deconstruction is something that we all must do more of. We must pull apart this field and question its parts, contexts, and meanings so that we can engage in dialogue that prepares us to respond to the inevitably greater uncertainty, ambiguity, and complexity of the future. Some of our ideas about DEI may no longer serve us. Others may need a reframing and amplification with new meaning and actions toward sustainability.

I believe that if we, as practitioners and advocates, don't purposefully deconstruct DEI now, critics will. And the result of those critiques will fuel outcomes that are opposite of those that committed practitioners aspire to.

Some people think DEI is getting too much focus. A survey of 6,275 American workers done by Momentive (previously SurveyMonkey) in 2021 showed that 51 percent of white C-level executives say that DEI initiatives are a distraction from their company's "real work." In the same survey, 36 percent of Hispanic senior managers and 26 percent of Black middle managers also felt that DEI initiatives are a distraction.

Conversely, the Momentive survey states that 72 percent of entry-level workers believe that DEI initiatives are an important factor in their companies' success, with 62 percent of the entire survey population agreeing. Why the difference between younger workers and C-level executives? What makes some Black and Hispanic managers feel DEI initiatives are a distraction? Questions like these are at the heart of a mindset of deconstruction. The answers would surely not be binary—people's opinions are more complex than that. One's rationale for their perception could be anything from not agreeing with the focus of DEI efforts to finding what is being done inaccessible, to not trusting that the efforts as practiced will be meaningful to themselves or to the organization. If we are consistently incisive in our exploration and inquiry, we create space for inclusion to win for everyone.

Time for Reconstruction

I am writing this book because diversity, equity, and inclusion has never been more vital for organizations. But despite this growing importance, there have been very few frameworks to advance the work beyond historical attachment to representation. Words like "belonging" and "equity" have been added to the aspirational outcomes, but the pathways to make this accessible, actionable, and sustainable have not matched the aspirations. With such enthusiasm, it is possible that this is our last and best chance to save DEI from death by a thousand platitudes.

Reconstruction is a term that we have heard throughout history. Most Americans associate it with the policy enacted after the Civil War. New policies and US constitutional amendments created the way for the abolishment of slavery, citizenship to all born on American soil, and enfranchisement for Black men (all men). Then, the gains were lost with policies and inaction that led to a deleterious outcome: Jim Crow. As scholar and public intellectual W. E. B. Du Bois framed it: "The slave went free; stood a brief moment in the sun," but in a cloud of indifference "a new slavery arose."

Perhaps the second attempt at Reconstruction in America happened during the Civil Rights movement. Political and economic gains came in the form of the Civil Rights Act of 1964 and the Voting Rights Act of 1965, along with the previous desegregation of schools. Federal funds were allocated to programs designed to elevate Black Americans out of poverty and expand the middle class.

Unfortunately, this didn't last either. A new more subtle and insidious resistance emerged. It used legal intervention and interpretation with the intent to maintain or embolden economic dominance. With the gains made by Blacks during the Civil Rights era (1954–1968), the "southern strategy" circled back to a zero-sum framing by conservatives that pulled lower-middle-class and poor whites into believing that the gains of Blacks equaled a loss for them. A similar argument was made by anti-abolitionists, and some people still believe this today.[1] The argument that equitable societies lead to a win-lose dynamic was not right or true in the past, nor will it be in the future. What it does and is doing (mostly unintentionally) is presenting DEI, once again—despite diversity wheels showing myriad diversity dimensions, focusing on inclusion, and hoping to create organizations where all people belong—as heavily focused on race.

This reminds us again that an identity-by-identity approach (i.e., most acutely Black racial identity and, due to subsequent tragedies, Asian racial identity) doesn't, as it tends to be framed, serve everyone. Dismantling racism and racial justice are critically important outcomes that we must work toward. Simultaneously, we must be intentional about whether we are making such conversations and actions related to DEI accessible to everyone. Doing so can accelerate and foster the reconstruction—post-pandemic, global, and urgent—that humanity so desperately needs.

Reconstructing inclusion is about reimagining and formulating actionable ideas that can collectively elevate humanity. The ideas of this book are like active ingredients in a potion.

I propose a reconstructed paradigm to make inclusiveness accessible (for everyone), actionable (unambiguously prioritized), and sustainable (aligned with organizational purpose). The idea is to create greater alignment so that DEI efforts add value to entire organizations. That means all members, regardless of their identity or beliefs. We need everyone in our organizations speaking openly and taking action, adding value and creating organizational impact using the tools and skills of diversity, equity, and inclusion.

While purposefully deconstructing—breaking down and becoming more familiar with concepts related to DEI in the following chapters (e.g., meritocracy, intersectionality, exclusion)—the non-exhaustive framing and reframing of these ideas will then move toward illustrating and expanding on what I call an "Inclusion System."

At the center of *Reconstructing Inclusion* are these questions: If diversity and inclusion were deconstructed and then reconstructed again, how can they be reconstructed to make inclusion accessible, actionable, and sustainable? How can organizations make inclusion normative?

An Inclusion System provides guidance on the conditions critical to making inclusion normative in a sense that it is accessible to all organizational stakeholders. *Accessible* in this sense means inclusion is not a shallow idea that connotes that its worth is only for marginalized identities but is meaningful and helpful to everyone. *Actionable* means that inclusion is unambiguously prioritized and designed into organizational systems and structures. And *sustainable* connotes that inclusion is aligned with organizational purpose. Sustainability for me is about the entire organizational ecosystem. Being aligned with purpose is about positively contributing to the organization, its current and future members, and the communities and geographies in which it currently does and hopes to do business for generations to come.

Reconstructing Inclusion is an expedition into and through the field of diversity and inclusion. The focus of the book is *inclusion*, which is not an opposite to its antonym (*exclusion*) in this context. Rather, inclusion is *a set of tools, skills, and behaviors that create the conditions for all organizational stakeholders to thrive.*

By reconstructing inclusion, we create a new way forward. It starts with taking an honest inventory of where we are as a field. Most scholars would say that any attempt at reconstruction in the historical sense, even in the current sense of what is needed as we emerge from COVID-19, requires truth, reconciliation, and regeneration. *Reconstructing Inclusion* is influenced by this idea. Perhaps the distinction is that what we need now is not only a reconstruction focused on the United States. We need to move toward a global humanist scaffolding for community and planetary reconstruction.

After the journey into a non-exhaustive deconstruction, I describe an "Inclusion System." Following the discussion about developing an Inclusion System, I will explore the critical components that are needed if an organization desires to build such an entity.

Let's proceed in deconstructing, and then reconstructing, inclusion.

Diversity Is . . .

> "Indeed, diversity has become virtually a sacred concept in American life today. No one's really against it; people tend instead to differ only in their degrees of enthusiasm for it and their ingenuity in pursuing it."
>
> **—Walter Benn Michaels,** *The Trouble with Diversity*[1]

In past presentations at conferences and workshops, I have turned to the audience to ask them to respond when I flash a slide that reads, "Diversity Is . . ." The responses depend on where I am, who I am with, and how much experience the audience has with the subject. The most common answer has been about representation. When I inquire into why this matters, the responses have included convictions about equality and equity; beliefs about the moral thing to do; and, from those well versed in the diversity literature from consulting firms, "business case" statistics that have been challenged by researchers who are clearly supporters of DEI.[2] I conclude this dialogue with audiences by stating that diversity is inevitable—it's what we do with it that makes the difference.

Sometimes when I listen to fellow DEI practitioners use their jargon, I think we sound like aliens from another universe inviting those from Earth, where we have recently arrived, to a meal. We set the table with our unfamiliar dishes and expect the Earthlings to all be instantly enthusiastic about the otherworldly plates of . . . something ill-defined and foreign suddenly placed in front of them.

If we want colleagues at our metaphorical dinner party to trust and sample our offerings, we need to set the table in an inviting manner. The best way is to prepare the meal *with* Earthlings. If that's not possible, the second-best way is to talk with the colleagues ahead of the meal about their taste preferences and dietary needs and do our best to be accommodating. The next best approach is probably to invite them for tea or coffee and share things that are familiar to them. Eventually, we create a level of trust and curiosity about the delights from our respective kitchens.

At age 28, I decided to stop eating meat. I didn't completely stop eating animal products, but I drastically diminished my intake of things that were born of a mother and slaughtered. This perplexed my mother to such a degree that she began to talk to everyone about the fact that I didn't eat meat anymore: "You know, Amri is a vegetarian now." My family, being from Kansas City, which is known for its barbeque, figured it was because I hadn't been tempted by Gates (a well-known local barbeque restaurant/brand) frequently enough. They concluded that the next time I returned home for a visit and saw everyone licking Gates's famous sauce off their fingers, I would get such an overwhelming craving that I would immediately launch into a juicy rib, and the world would be back to normal. Their son, nephew, cousin would be rescued from the alien world of the no-meat eaters.

More than twenty years later, my commitment to not eating sentient beings (and a few other things that can make it equally difficult for someone not experienced in how I eat to cook for me) remains, and I am resolved to maintain this lifestyle without compromise. What I have never done is expect anyone to follow what I have chosen to do or require them to accommodate me if they find it too challenging. Although I have met many people who decided to become vegetarian for a variety of reasons, including some like mine, during their period of inquiry, I've shared the context for my transformation only when asked.

Many mothers take feeding their children seriously. My mother is no different. In the years after I finished graduate school and started working, there were fewer opportunities for me to visit home. When I did come home, my mother wanted to prepare food for me. She wanted to prepare *her food* for me. One day when I was home in Topeka, in the kitchen where we spent a good deal of time together, she said, "You can't eat all the things that I raised you on." It broke my heart.

At that moment, it became clear to me that becoming vegetarian was not just about me. It was about her and my community at large. Context—or lack thereof—is at the root of almost every misunderstanding, conflict, and decision that we make. In the work we have been doing in DEI for the past five decades, we have thrown countless hours and loads of energy into sharing *our context*; that is, the background and perspective of the practitioner and all our data justifying why what we are trying to do is so important. Where we often fail is in exercising perspective-taking ourselves.

Perspective-taking is not a skill that switches on automatically once we turn five and remains active thereafter. Instead, it is more like a car engine that must be started every time it's needed. Failing to turn on our perspective-taking when needed—perhaps because of lack of attention, time, or motivation—can easily cause our reasoning to stall. To move toward a better understanding of others' viewpoints, we need to actively turn on our perspective-taking skills.[3]

Some have framed this idea as a type of empathy and coupled it with emotional intelligence (EQ). To understand and feel what the other is feeling is powerful. To walk in their shoes is a noble aspiration. Empathy is great when one can get it. However, the reality is that if we empathize and the feelings of the so-called other are not feelings that we prefer, how easily do we simultaneously hold such contradictory sentiments?

Perspective-taking is more actionable and more likely to create a win-win situation. I may not know how you feel, and you may or may not be able or be comfortable to tell me. Nonetheless, if I am practicing perspective-taking, I can learn where you're coming from and respond in a manner that enables gradual adjustments to be made in how we share our contexts. From there, we can create a greater willingness to being influenced by each other. As practitioners, how good are we at this?

My perspective-taking allowed my mother and me to rethink her traditional dishes with a few substitutions that maintained the flavor and allowed me to devour them like I did as a child.

Isn't *Everything* Diversity?

In 2017, twenty-year Apple veteran Denise Young Smith was part of a panel in Bogotá, Colombia. She had recently taken on a formal role as VP of Inclusion and Diversity after several other senior roles. During the questions from the moderator, she said the following:

> And I've often told people a story—there can be twelve white blue-eyed blonde men in a room, and they are going to be diverse too because they're going to bring a different life experience and life perspective to the conversation. The issue is representation and mix and bringing all the voices into the room that can contribute to the outcome of any situation. So I focus on everyone, but I also focus on allies and alliances because to [the other panelists'] point, there's an incredible amount of power in those who have platforms or those who have the benefit of greater representation to tell the stories of those who do not.[4]

Ms. Smith was castigated for fewer than fifty words (italicized above) of a full response that both qualified and clarified her story. The result: after twenty years in the company, she resigned. Clearly, where so-called diversity advocates are concerned, Smith crossed the line. Due to the reputational impact to Apple, she had to step down from a company that obviously held great significance to her. Was this a win for the DEI supporters? Why didn't Apple support her statement, reinforcing the idea that diversity is about everyone? I cannot answer for Apple's leadership. Maybe if Steve Jobs had still been living, he would have agreed and created a public dialogue. Who knows?

What I do know is that Ms. Smith was right.

About every facet of a person's identity, background, experience, and preferences can be placed under the label of "diversity." If you have been in a diversity training, you may have seen a diversity wheel. In case you haven't, they look something like this:

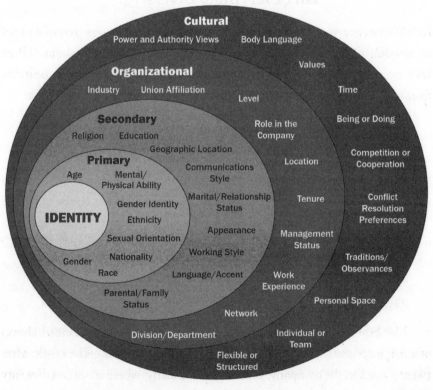

Figure 1

There is a great deal of variety in this wheel. If you were trying to find out the various aspects of how you would describe yourself—from how you describe your physical appearance all the way through the cultural values you might exhibit as a result of your family culture—you could get pretty close to identifying a majority of personal aspects. If you see Figure 1 as a graphical version of all types of human beings, it's easy to feel that everything is "diversity." Going by the image above, all of our distinctions are relevant and part of how individuals can be considered when we practice DEI. At the same time, diversity can suffer from the priority curse, as in, "When everything is a priority, then nothing is." If we replace "priority" with "diversity," are all of the above diversity or simply aspects of individuals and teams? Why even use the term "diversity"?

The representation of underrepresented groups in business has been consistently below the often-cited percentages that reflect the population of women and minorities in the US.[5] How those population-based percentage markers came to be the optimal proportions for organizations to aspire to hasn't been thoroughly researched.[6] It's likely that someone made them up, similar to a lot of the things that have been assumed as "best practices" in the field. Smith was right that there are various types of differences among any group of people, including those that *appear* phenotypically homogenous. What she could not have anticipated is that people who seemingly have the same objectives as her would attack her simply because of her choice of words.

How much good was gained for DEI when Denise Young Smith, a tenured senior HR leader, who happens to be a Black woman, at one of the most powerful companies in the world, resigned after public sentiment determined that she "just didn't get it" because of a single true statement? In the words of the iconic Edwin Starr, "War, huh, good God. What is it good for? Absolutely nothing, listen to me." Diversity gained nothing and may have lost something. I'm sure Ms. Smith is thriving in her new roles. My hope is that those who decided to attack a colleague for voicing the idea that white men are also part of the diversity conversation will reflect on the negative impacts of their reactions.

The Language of DEI

Another place where progress (at least as it relates to accessibility) has been slowed is in the terminology of diversity. Consider the words in Table 1 below. The list isn't in any particular order, and isn't exhaustive, but it is relatively extensive. Are these words accessible to most people in the world? Not at all.

Oppression	Racial Justice	Transphobia	Anti-racist/ Antiracism	They/Them
Gender Fluidity	Belonging	Gender Spectrum	Intersectional Feminism	BIPOC
Microaggression	Womanx	Equity vs. Equality	Intersectionality	LGBTQIA++
Unearned Privilege	White Supremacy Culture	Allyship	Heteronormative	Latinx

Table 1. Diversity, Equity, and Inclusion Jargon

One of my tests of accessibility is whether my mother would understand. She holds a PhD from Kansas State University, has lived in Kansas (Topeka and Kansas City) her whole life, is what I would call a social justice–oriented center-right conservative, and used to teach diversity to undergraduate education students. My mother hadn't heard of most of these words. And when I asked her to tell me what the ones she had heard of meant, she said she didn't know or provided an incomplete explanation. I then asked my wife. English is her sixth language. She was born and raised by Spanish parents in the French-speaking part of Switzerland, she is politically agnostic, and she has worked for a global corporation and been active in diversity initiatives for several years. Her initial response for most of them was, "I have no idea what many of these words mean. I can make sense of some of them at face value, but don't know the meaning of most of them." Neither of the women closest to me are alone.

I recall the first time I read the term "womxn," which is used to designate the entire spectrum of those people who identify as women whether they were born with all XX chromosomes or not. Being (what I used to think was) "woke," I thought I had seen all of the terms. Turns out, I was wrong (not so "woke") and continue to be introduced to new terms regularly. It may be that I am aging out of knowing the latest slang terms—diversity-related or not—but I did eventually get "meh," "on fleek," "IG," "bootylicious," and recently along with womxn, "vidushi," even though I may not get any other terms Beyoncé or other influencers might be introducing to the world.

Having an industry-specific jargon isn't new. Every company I have worked with has had its own terms. Those terms could be the same as another firm and have different meanings. Within the company, the various functions have their own language emerging from their subculture. They have inside jokes and references that are unlikely to be understood by those not in the in-group. This is a natural, organic result of self-organizing.

Given the intentions of our work as DEI practitioners, we would have more success if we made our language accessible to everyone. Many of the terms we loosely and at times indiscriminately use, too often to make the so-called other wrong, are counterproductive. In fact, some terms from the list above (which will be discussed later) have been politically weaponized to serve as terms of contention versus language that creates a collective understanding about how we can navigate the complex distinctions that can hinder and/or add value to organizational life.

Ecosystems

Who doesn't love a ripe, sweet, creamy banana? Worldwide banana crops are a $12 billion industry, and in some countries, bananas account for up to 27 percent of calorie consumption. Despite the breadth, nutritional benefits, and economic need for banana crops to be sustained, they are currently at risk due to monoculture.

Most bananas on the market are of the Cavendish variety. They emerged from the greenhouse of a duke in northern England, grown by his gardener, Joseph Paxton, who discovered the Cavendish and imported them from Mauritius in the 1830s. They were named Musa Cavendishii after the Duke's family name, William George Spencer Cavendish. Cavendish bananas make up about half of worldwide exports.[7]

The Cavendish banana replaced the Gros Michel, also known as "Big Mike," in the 1950s when the Gros Michel was blighted by a black fungus called Panama disease. Exporters of banana crops needed to discover a species that mimicked, as closely as possible, the qualities that allowed the Gros Michel to be shipped all over the world, and they did. That was— until the 1990s, when a new fungal threat emerged, first discovered in Taiwan and currently found in most tropical countries where the Cavendish is grown. This threat is the result of monoculture. That is, Cavendish bananas are the only bananas grown in many plantations, meaning that if one variety is planted and is susceptible to a disease, all of the plants are ruined. Monoculture is well known as an agricultural problem. It was responsible for the great potato famine of the Irish from 1845–1849 that was responsible for approximately one million deaths and millions of people emigrating from Ireland.

There are more than a thousand different varieties of bananas grown in the world. It begs the question, if food scientists and farmers know the risks of monoculture, why do they continue to perpetuate it? With so many varieties to choose from, why not just rotate them or plant multiple types on one plantation? The answer is more complex than it appears.

The demand for bananas is high. Most varieties of bananas are grown and eaten locally. Many of those varieties would not be suitable for long-distance travel after harvest. Luckily for those of us who are not living in an area where bananas can grow, we have access to the Cavendish (for now).

For a banana to travel to Europe, it has to be shipped from Africa or Asia (and in some cases Australia). To do so, it must be picked when it is completely green, much greener than what we call "green" when we purchase them, so it can ripen in our kitchens. Bananas require transport at a temperature that doesn't require massive amounts of costly refrigeration, and they have to be edible and tasty enough; that is, they cannot have seeds (or at least not be seeded when consumed and contain little pulp). When you combine all these variables, the Cavendish becomes the only variety that consistently meets the criteria. Therefore, companies that produce bananas for export have thrived on monoculture. Monoculture isn't desired, but it meets a need and has its benefits . . . until it doesn't.

Organizations can unintentionally evolve as monocultures, too. Organizational monocultures can take the form of fixed ways and traditions that people believe the organization must continue. Organizational monocultures cultivate what a small group of influential individuals has determined to constitute success. They articulate and incentivize what needs to be done, and deviations generally have negative consequences. Most modern organizations would shun this type of setup, yet it is likely that somewhere in any organization of more than a hundred people, a monocultural orientation is forming.

Organizational monocultures are easy to recognize if one looks closely enough. A manager is hiring team members with characteristics (at least cognitively) that are similar to each other. Those members are referring their friends. The team seems to operate well. In fact, you may be seeing a short-term performance burst. Beyond people hired, external relationships revolve around the same players; critical information sharing is limited to the privileged; there is little to no dissent in team meetings; people are not caring for or intentionally helping teammates get better; non-core team members and colleagues have not been invited to team meetings and are not openly asked for input. But things are efficient; people *seem* happy; turnover is lower than it has been in years; numbers are being hit; and people are being rewarded for doing so. Their monocultural orientation is working, until it changes abruptly (monocultures, like monocrops, can collapse suddenly) and business starts to suffer.

Diversity, however, can prevent the perpetuation of monocultures before an organization experiences the inevitable extinction events that occur biologically and organizationally. Monocultures often can produce in abundance, as in the Cavendish example. However, if an organization wants sustainable growth—the intentional cultivation of diversity is not optional.

Cultivating a monoculture will eventually always negatively impact the bottom line. Your best people will leave because they don't see space being created for a broad variety of employees and their respective perspectives. Others, upon getting word of a culture where a certain phenotype (i.e., including and beyond physical appearances) predominates, will lose affinity for your company. As a result, even potential talent will opt out of considering employment with your firm.

Like bananas, organizations have only small windows to benefit from monoculture. Those that recognize that the antidote is diversity (cognitive and identity) will create an organizational culture where people seek out and have cultivated a willingness to be influenced by their neighbors. Those who don't will likely end up like the Gros Michel banana crops of the 1950s. Extinct.

Diversity Drives Innovation

Before there was a maddening drive toward the aspiration of "digital transformation," every company with any prospects for growth was locked in on innovation. How do we innovate? What is the secret sauce for innovation? What does it take to generate the formula to unlock all of the innovation potential in an organization? Nothing was considered more important.

One leading innovation scholar, the late Harvard professor Clayton Christensen, wrote many books on innovation. Two of them that stand out for DEI practitioners are *The Innovator's Dilemma*, where he describes the paradox—or, as he frames it, the "dilemma"—of the innovator,[8] and *The Innovator's DNA*, where he and his co-authors, professors Jeff Dyer and Hal Gregersen, discuss the behaviors that allow innovation to thrive at the individual and organizational level.

The Innovator's Dilemma discusses how expertly trained, highly skilled, and competent managers try and fail despite making decisions using all the techniques they have been trained to use. One particular reason why companies often fail to create new disruptive technologies is that they are customer dependent. They focus on what customers say more so than what they do. Christensen, in one of his case studies, indicates that he would watch carefully what customers do, not simply listen to what they say. He says, "Watching how customers actually use a product provides much more reliable information than can be gleaned from a verbal interview or a focus group."

Where diversity is concerned, DEI practitioners have a great deal of experience engaging leaders and teams within the organizations we have worked with. After working with teams and people leaders in talent reviews (performance and/or succession), training/education, team facilitation, and beyond, the responses are generally positive. Some teams and leaders even talk about follow-up possibilities. Several of them verbally committed to the ideas discussed. The question is, what do people do in between one DEI engagement and the next? Many times, we cannot say.

One of the most impactful interventions I ever did for teams was long-term team observation. This consisted of at least two people from my team sitting in on high-level decision-making meetings and coding the participation by type—inquiry, advocacy, acknowledgment, and a set of behaviors that we assembled from the literature and defined as best we could so that we would be looking for the same types of behaviors. After observing these decision-making bodies (some of which operated as teams and others as a collection of individual functional subject matter experts), we would present the collected data to them with the intent of them seeing their behaviors. The feedback included observation data to build awareness of how they interacted with each other, as well as insights from those who came to present and have decisions made about their project. Obviously, our being present brought about some changes in behavior. Nonetheless, we saw that, over time, the groups made decisions about *how* and why they needed to change their behaviors in meetings. Some even made changes in the process that made presenters feel more welcomed, confident, and able to disagree and debate, which power imbalances often prohibited.

Those teams were our clients. We listened to them and what they said they wanted. They originally wanted us to do training. We eventually did.

Yet, we didn't just do *a training*, as most diversity training doesn't work.[9] Rather, we observed what they did over time. Then, with the information we gathered, we created sessions that consisted of not only information delivery but also information exchange and co-creation. The disruption, if we can call it that, was self-generated and therefore actionable. While many of the groups changed their composition during the roughly two years that we observed and worked with these teams, we saw them implement process changes that created structures for what they wanted more of: bolder presentations by project leaders, faster decisions, and more open dialogue.

Christensen's *The Innovator's DNA* speaks to the behaviors that great innovators exhibit and codifies their behaviors[10]—behaviors that inherently require a willingness to be open to diverse perspectives from broad networks of people: 1) associating (the ability to make surprising connections across areas of knowledge, industries, even geographies); 2) questioning (crafting and asking skillful and probing questions to better understand what is and what might be); 3) observing (carefully watching what goes on near and far; seeing how things work and often how they do not work); 4) networking (devoting time and energy to finding and testing ideas through a network of diverse individuals); and 5) experimenting (generating data on what might work in the future). We could even call these behaviors of inclusion.

Diversity has too often left us in a reductionist state of mind. That is, our focus on the representation of specific identities may be a self-inflicted barrier to collective progress. Fervent advocacy for single identity groups—the heightened concentration on anti-racism for the benefit of Black people, for example—may be narrowing the prospects for bending the curve of inequity.[11]

Reducing diversity to particular attributes is contrary even to the sensibilities of the most awakened social justice warrior. Yet, our reactionary natures may be getting the best of us (much as they did with the forced resignation of Denise Young Smith). The complexity we face in life and in our organizations reflects humanity (the superset), of which our identities (subsets) play a role. And none of those roles are played alone.

3

Identity and Choice?

"When I discover who I am, I'll be free."

—**Ralph Ellison,** *Invisible Man*

My first exposure to cognitive and unconscious bias as a working professional was in 2003. My mentor and business partner asked me to go to the website of Harvard's Project Implicit and take a few tests.

I took the first test, and the outcome came back stating: "Your data suggest a strong automatic preference for Light Skinned vs. Dark Skinned people." At the time, my work had me occupying offices in the Washington, DC, metro area and Atlanta. The two cities where I spent most of my time had two of the largest Black populations in the US. I figured that I'm "dark skinned people," and so are most of the people I consider part of my close circle. They aren't all Black people, but they would not qualify as "light skinned people" according to the visual description in the skin-tone Implicit Association Test (IAT) on the Harvard Project Implicit website.

Upon receiving this result, I quickly went to my colleague's office and said, "The test is broken." He said, "It's broken, huh? It has never seemed broken to me. What happened?" I explained that it said that I preferred light-skinned people over dark-skinned people, and that obviously wasn't true, and that it must be that I wasn't used to using the keyboard in the manner they suggested. He smiled and suggested that I take it again.

I did. My results after slowing down and trying to be as accurate as I could said: "Your data suggest a moderate automatic preference for Light Skinned vs. Dark Skinned people." Both results left me a bit miffed until I understood that there are so many reasons why I may have scored that way, reasons ranging from the fact that my family has a range of hues (the majority who are racially Black) to the reality that most people I encountered in a day through my work were light-skinned. I acknowledged that my long-term (via my family) and short-term exposure were likely to have colored my perception.

For many years since, I've regularly taken IATs. At the time of the story above, and up until 2020, I was doing a lot of classroom unconscious bias training. I wanted to stay fresh and familiar with changes on the website, new research, and other evolutions. I took two or three IATs per week on average for many years. In that time, I saw my preference toward young versus old change. Jimmie, a sixty-seven-year-old retired fireman at my gym who could more than double the number of pull-ups I was able to do, changed my perception. Although my association with old wasn't negative, I did believe that older people were weaker. Jimmie was far from weak.

My perception of Jimmie's face as "old" to me, and my idea that he was weak, persisted until one day when I was lifting heavy weights and he was the only person available to spot me. He spotted (assisted) me, making it look easy. From that day on, when I had a chance to share a station with him (like pull-ups) or have him spot me, I took it. My IAT scores went from having a strong automatic preference for "Young People vs. Older People" to neutral in my preference. Why?

After my experience with Jimmie, I intentionally looked for examples of other people I considered to look "older," like the way I framed Jimmie, who were also taking on a physical activity that required above average strength. Seeing people in their sixties and seventies doing things such as heavy weight training, intense body-weight exercises, and playing soccer (football) at a moderate game pace qualified them and, I believe, subtly changed my perception.

Fast-forward to late 2019. I took the IAT for "Light Skin vs. Dark Skin," and for the first time in many attempts, my results said: "Your data suggest a strong automatic preference for Dark Skinned vs. Light Skinned people." It was the opposite result I expected, especially since I no longer live in a "Chocolate City"—I live in Switzerland. There is a lot of chocolate here, but not a large percentage of chocolate-skinned people. I am married to a light-skinned Spanish woman, and my stepchildren are light-skinned Swiss. The only people who would be described as darker skinned are my son and myself. And looking at my son, he is not what one would label as "dark-skinned"; more like an almond with hues of Bronze, Desert Sand, and Gel Fx Rose (per Crayola™).

My exposure in Switzerland to dark-skinned people has been minimal at best, and my most recent IAT reveals that I prefer dark-skinned people more than any other test I have taken. I am not saddened or upset by the results. I love people who look (color-wise) like me, but not any more or less than I love my family members (and those go beyond my wife, who, while Spanish, is close in skin tone to some of my relatives who identify racially as Black).

Litigating the reasons why my most recent IAT changed is more complex than I can tackle in this space. Such complexity lies inside of the socioeconomic construct that is race.

Heterogeneity

No matter what one thinks of Rachel Dolezal, there is no denying that her story opened up a conversation rife with sentiment (at least in the US) that cut across cultural lines and revealed racially uniform, aligned, or homogeneous opinions. You could say that the topic of Rachel Dolezal (who gained acclaim as for being racially classified as white but who identifies culturally in a manner that caused most of her associates to assume she was Black) was an inclusive opening. One writer said, "She is in some ways a Rorschach test. She is that person that depending on who you are, and where you sit, and your lens, you will react to her differently."[1]

Personally, I was a bit perplexed by the argument. Note: I am Black and proud to be part of the culture. I didn't need to say that. But given that it's possible some people reading this book or this passage will potentially question my motivation, I wanted to make it clear.

I was left puzzled because I wasn't sure what Rachel Dolezal did "wrong" that made her the target of Black people. I was more certain about why she garnered sympathy from white women, some of whom envy stereotypical and archetypical characteristics that are often associated with Black women. That was easy. In fact, if we look at the sociocultural trends in what is considered beautiful, being like a "strong, smart black woman" (SSBW) is what I would say many women might desire to emulate, in theory. Considering the circumstances, the cliché of the SSBW is a desired way of being in all of its hyperbolic reality.

Rachel Dolezal made several choices. The choices did not seem to be altogether deliberate. Her context, affinities, and preferences brought her to them. Dolezal was born as a racially classified white woman from Montana. During her life, particularly during her teens and twenties, she had developed such a connection with African American/Black culture and communities that she began to (at least implicitly) identify as a Black woman to the communities in which she lived and worked.

Let's say we described a random woman who lived in Jackson, Mississippi, for several years, went to Howard University (a historically Black university), has three Black sons (one of them adopted), was former president of a local Washington State chapter of the National Association for the Advancement of Colored People (NAACP), and taught African and African American history at two different colleges. She wears box braids and other Afrocentric hairstyles. How would you picture her? What kinds of conversations would you have with her? How would you relate to her if you didn't know she was "the white woman that passed for Black"? For me, it would be an absolute shock to hear about the above person and then see her classified as a white woman. She sounds more Afrocentric than me.

The argument lies in the fact that Rachel Dolezal *did* feel confident in her identity. It's likely part of the problem that many people, including what Dolezal might describe as "other Black women," have with what she did.

Cultural (mis)appropriation (another word for the diversity glossary of terms) was the description many used.[2] Others took her to be disingenuous, not acknowledging that her white-skinned privilege made her feel empowered to conveniently "pretend to be Black."

What is palpable when reading tweets and articles from Black women is confounding emotions and the resonance of the pain body[3] in observing what may be viewed as an intruder without legitimacy or authenticity looking to possess "the only thing that we cannot have taken away from us, even if we desired to have done so." Yet, this woman can take on being Black just as white actors and actresses have done in television and film for decades, portraying Native Americans, Blacks, Asians, you name it. Or those who studied Black music and then made (and continue to make via royalties and touring) large sums of money using styles and rhythms that they acquired listening to these Black artists who were making a relative pittance. It is understandable. At the same time, I don't know if what Dolezal did was wrong.

In 1997, Tiger Woods, a once-in-a-generation phenomenon of a golfer, won the Masters Golf Tournament. The 1997 victory was his first of five wins of the tournament, including being the reigning champion at the inception of me writing this book. Woods is of mixed heritage. His mother is of Thai and Chinese descent, and his late father is of mixed ancestry, including Caribbean, African, Native American, and Caucasian. When Woods won the '97 Masters and the media claimed him as the first African American to win the event, it bothered him. He was proud of the heritage that came from his parents. All of that heritage, he felt, should be acknowledged. Woods, with the intention of articulating to the public how he sees himself and perhaps suggesting how we should see him, suggested a new term that could perhaps only apply to himself. That term, "Cablinasian" (referring to the mixed ancestry above), at the time was seemingly reserved for Tiger.

However, there are likely quite a few people who could metaphorically check all the same boxes that Tiger checks. They might use the term "Blackanese" or the more general Black and Asian combination, "Blasian," which is generally accepted in the Black community. Perhaps Woods shouldn't have thrown in that his father has Native American heritage. A lot of Black Americans claim to have Native American heritage. But, in fact, that range of Black people with actual First Nations' heritage is 0.6 to 2 percent.

There are other lesser known cases from DNA testing companies where people were shocked about the findings. Some people were disappointed that they had African in them. Others were shocked that they had so little. Sigrid Johnson was raised as a Black child with racially mixed parents who identified as Black. Her parents were lighter skinned, so Johnson assumed that her lighter hue resulted from her parents' mixed ancestry. She found out as a teenager that she was adopted and that her birth mother was white. It turns out that she was the child of a mixed-race extramarital affair, and the husband of her Italian mother couldn't bear raising a darker-skinned child, particularly one from his wife's lover. So, she still believed that she was mixed.

What Ms. Johnson discovered from her test was that genetically she was hardly African at all. Her results: 45.306 percent Hispanic, 32.321 percent Middle Eastern, 13.714 percent European, and 8.659 percent "other," which included a mere 2.978 percent African. Other DNA testing beyond the 23andMe snapshot above yielded less certain results, with confidence intervals ranging from 0 to 54 percent for all African ancestry categories. Although the likelihood that her results were significantly different from the other tests was low, she was still satisfied by the possibility for a higher percentage despite remaining perplexed about the results. As she was eagerly and a bit nervously waiting for the results, Johnson said, "You know, even if the results are the same as they were before, *I am still a Black woman.*"

Interestingly, the percentage of European DNA among people identifying as African American ranges between 19–29 percent with the same set of tests. Dr. Henry Louis Gates Jr., who has offered that "Black culture is a trope," says in an article for *The Root* that, "A whopping 35 percent of all African-American men descend from a white male ancestor who fathered a mulatto child sometime in the slavery era, most probably from rape or coerced sexuality." Further, "it turns out that black people in this country are surprisingly 'white,' meaning that our genomes are composed of quite a lot of European ancestry. Judging from these test results, the bottom line is that black and white Americans are inextricably interconnected at the level of their genomes, and African Americans are a profoundly 'mixed' people, far more than anyone thought possible before these DNA tests were invented."[4]

Two questions that Rachel Dolezal presents in the Netflix documentary *The Rachel Divide* are a recurring theme in the stories of Woods and Johnson as well. One can imagine they are of critical interest for all who believe that "bringing one's authentic self to work" is important. Dolezal posits, "Who's the gatekeeper for Blackness? . . . Do we actually have the right to live how we feel?"[5] I would add, who is the gatekeeper for any of our chosen and/or acquired identities?

While the circumstances differed, all of the above people (Dolezal, Woods, and Johnson) chose how they wanted to be identified. One went on genetics. The others based it on their significant influences, whether outside of original context (Dolezal) or the result of the context selected for them (Johnson). Woods chose to invoke "all" of his identity and was told by the Black community, in relatively certain terms, that "you are ours." He was even expressly told who he must pledge allegiance to by those in the community who clearly know race has no biological basis. The rationale is that "Blacks are already short on role models; we cannot share them with others." I made that up, but I am searching for why a community would reject someone who is actively contributing to its improvement with altruistic intentions. Dolezal took on the presidency of the Spokane NAACP and sat on various community boards. At a minimum, Dolezal built significant social capital and, for what it's worth, there is no racial or cultural requirement to do this.

Woods and Dolezal are not unlike any of us at various points in our lives as we define ourselves. "We seek out and cultivate identities to fill our need to belong, and it's through that lens of identity that we see and understand the world," said Jay Van Bavel, a psychology professor at New York University who researches how group identities, values, and beliefs shape the mind and brain.[6] "So, when you get information that challenges your identity, many people tune it out, just like we do with headlines and news stories when they counter our politics and belief system." Johnson decided to tune hers out and go with what she'd known for sixty-two years. Maybe the gatekeepers of Blackness, Hispanicness, Middle Easternness, and so on should contact her about who she claims to be after her genetic test clearly demonstrated that *she is not* the identity *that she has chosen*.

How is this an argument that can ever be resolved?

Inclusion as Systems Thinking

Peter Senge, an organizational scientist and the author of *The Fifth Discipline: The Art & Practice of the Learning Organization*, defines "systems thinking" as the discipline that pulls all others together and enables the flourishing of a learning organization. The five disciplines of a learning organization, including systems thinking, are:[7]

1. **Personal mastery:** The discipline of continually clarifying and deepening our personal vision, of focusing our energies, of developing patience, and of seeing reality objectively.

2. **Mental models:** Deeply ingrained assumptions, generalizations, or even pictures or images that influence how we process and make sense of the world and how we act. These assumptions are such that we more than likely don't have conscious awareness of them or the effects they have on our behavior.

3. **Building shared vision:** The capacity to hold a shared vision of the future we seek to co-create. This includes learning the discipline of translating an "I" vision into a "we" vision. This is not a "cookbook" but a set of principles by which we work and live.

4. **Team learning:** "Thinking together" in dialogue is how Senge frames this discipline. Paulo Freire, the progressive Brazilian educator, gave conditions for dialogue including but not limited to trusting the "others," mutual respect and love (care and commitment), questioning what one knows, and knowing that, through dialogue, existing thoughts will change and new knowledge will be created.[8]

5. **Systems thinking:** "At the heart of a learning organization is a shift of mind—from seeing ourselves as separate from the world to connected to the world," says Senge. Systems thinking blends the above disciplines. It affirms that they are not used as buzzwords to satisfy a temporary need, particularly temporary needs that are not authentically oriented toward creating the sustainability of a learning organization.

Senge's work, while primarily concerned with how organizations learn to deal with the complexity of markets, emerging technologies, teams, and the individuals who contribute to teams in organizational life, surfaces many behaviors that either explicitly or expressly mirror inclusion. One framing that I have of inclusion is "intentional openness; a willingness to be influenced by the so-called 'other.'" When we look at the disciplines of Senge, we see elements of thinking together, trusting "others" as espoused by Freire to expound on team/group learning, a "we" development of vision rather than the "me" orientation.

Systems thinking, like diversity, equity, and inclusion, has been flooded with a variety of definitions over the years. The definition that Senge shares is one of the most prevalent: "a discipline for seeing wholes and a framework for seeing interrelationships rather than things, for seeing patterns of change rather than static snapshots." Computer science and engineering scholars

Ross Arnold and Jon Wade define it as "a set of synergistic analytic skills used to improve the capability of identifying and understanding systems, predicting their behaviors, and devising modifications to them in order to produce desired effects. These skills work together as a system." [9] They offer that their definition is perhaps the most accessible. When you read their micro-glossary, consider which of these behaviors, if any, you might deem to be inclusive.

Table 2 lists terms included in the Arnold and Wade definition of *systems thinking*:

Systems	Groups or combinations of interrelated, **interdependent**, or interacting elements forming collective entities.
Synergistic	Characteristic of **synergy**, which is the interaction of elements in a way that, when combined, **produce a total effect that is greater than the sum of the individual elements**.
Analytical skills	Skills that provide the ability to visualize, articulate, and **solve both complex and uncomplicated problems and concepts and make decisions that are sensible and based on available information**. Such skills include demonstration of the ability to apply logical thinking to gathering and analyzing information, designing and testing solutions to problems, and formulating plans.
Identify	To **recognize as being a particular thing**.
Understand	To be thoroughly familiar with; **apprehend clearly the character, nature, or subtleties of**.
Predict	To foretell as a deducible consequence.
Devise modifications	To contrive, plan, or elaborate **changes or adjustments**.

Table 2. Systems Thinking Terminology

In my experience, inclusion in action is fostered by a recognized necessity for interdependence. When it comes to synergy across differences, the collective set of cognitively distinctive tools produces more remarkable outcomes. The complex and the less involved problems are relative, with the diversity of those problems often presenting as more complex than originally understood—thus requiring a diversity of perspectives to make sound decisions. Inclusive practice consists of a variety of habits, skills, and actions that allow one to work through networks to understand and facilitate organizational cause and effect. That is, inclusion requires that one be familiar with feedback networks and be able to neutrally interpret the dynamics at play. Neutrality does not mean relying only on not having a personal opinion. Neutrality means that, with opinions in tow, there is a capability to *transmit what is learned for the purpose of [group] learning.* The purpose is not to get one to lean in a particular direction. Leanings or preferences (caused by a compelling cause or agenda or nudges from people's lived experiences and their stories) come later with and through dialogue.

DEI doesn't work without systems thinking. You don't have to formally design a system of inclusion for it to exist. DEI's effectiveness has been limited because, despite all that has gone into developing it, there has been too little rigorous effort to do ample inquiry into how we co-create a "total effect that is greater than the sum of the individual elements."

If there is something that is producing an outcome (mediocre or extraordinary), there is a system behind it. The likelihood that a system that is tied to a particular outcome and is part of another system is extremely high. What that means is that systems are always interrelated.

By chance, when extrapolating how connected a system like inclusion is, if you are overwhelmed at the depth or thinking that this is beyond your scope, remit, interest, budget, and/or capacity, that is reasonable. And it is likely the reason for thinking like this is that you may believe you must deal with the complexity alone. As shared before, DEI must be a "we" concept. As my career started in public health and healthcare, I often say that "the difference between 'illness' and 'wellness' is 'I' versus 'we.'" Dealing with the complexity by yourself will leave you sick and tired. This has been the experience of many of us doing this work. It doesn't have to be that way.

Acknowledging that systems are everyone's reality, where can the collective "we" make the biggest impact given that all that we do in our systems impacts everything? Further, if we conclude that inclusion is for everyone, and that a system for development is inclusive of everyone, "we maximize company productivity, profitability and long-term business success."[10]

For inclusion to work, systems thinking is required. For systems thinking to be optimal, inclusion is required.

The Urgency and Inevitability of Increasing Complexity

In 2015, leaders from 193 countries assembled to look at the state of global well-being in the world from drought, famine, war, plagues, and poverty. Their conclusion was that where we collectively stand in the world falls short of what is possible for humanity. They agreed that with the global resources available, poverty could be eliminated. Their belief that sustainable food production toward zero hunger, good health, and well-being are within reach was established and ratified. As a result of the discussions, the United Nations Sustainable Development Goals (SDG) were created.

The seventeen Sustainable Development Goals were created to address world economic, social, and environmental challenges that impacted global

progress given their direct and indirect impact on everyone living on our hyper-interdependent planet.

As can be seen in the seventeen goals in the graphic and the 169 objectives that can be found in the guiding document, the creators of the SDG were not only comprehensive in their scope, but also evoked urgency by giving stakeholders fifteen years to achieve this.[11]

They calculated that, with the resources available when creating the goals and the knowledge accessible at the time, the achievement of the goals was possible in many of their lifetimes.

Looking at this list, it is fairly clear that the level of complexity involved in realizing these seventeen goals and 169 objectives is far beyond any single person, organization, or government to understand and impact alone. In fact, the nature of the SDG conveys a message that things are more complex than ever seen in global history. If we don't act now, with a collective sense of urgency and clear direction, we will at best look back in history to a time on Earth and conclude that we failed to prepare the planet for our descendants. We failed to listen to a clear call to collective action, with our primary objective being that humanity is a choice that we make for the sake of self-preservation; and for the masses, a deep desire to see the world at peace for all children.

Complexity is inevitable, and given what we have just explored, it is not optional. It is not optional because, "Many of the challenges that we presently face—climate change, epidemics, terrorism, segregation, global economic disparities, financial markets, and international policy—involve complex systems. Each challenge involves anticipating and harnessing diverse, adaptive entities, with interdependent actions," says University of Michigan professor Scott Page.[12] Page's list seamlessly aligns with the seventeen SDGs and the 169 objectives. There is no disputing that interdependence is necessary, and given that inclusion operates at a systems and thus organizational level, any so-called attempts at inclusiveness without it would be incomplete at best.

The practice of DEI has led to many decisions that have inadvertently set precedents. These practices, in many instances based on acute reactions to tragic events or circumstances, unintentionally, in many cases, have created the opposite of what has been openly stated as a result of practicing inclusion. They have often conveyed, as in the response to the murder of George Floyd, that the purpose is for a particular subset of humanity, not everyone. I am not talking about right or wrong here; I am suggesting that we ask questions like, "How did this particular decision [related to something someone said or did to another person who self-identifies as being part of a subordinated group] help everyone grow to a greater understanding about inclusive behavior and leadership with an inclusive mindset?"

DEI's Potential for Transformation

At the root of my personal and spiritual philosophy is that we are all gifted with the possibility of transformation. It doesn't mean that it will happen automatically, but it still is in the realm of choice. This even applies to a young man accepted to Harvard, who later had his admission rescinded when his writings in Google Docs, in which he'd used a racial slur two years earlier, when he was sixteen years old, were discovered. Kyle Kashuv was a senior at Marjory Stoneman Douglas High School in southeast Florida, where seventeen of his schoolmates and teachers were left dead from a mass shooting in 2018. Kashuv emerged after the shooting, due to his views, as a vocal and prominent conservative figure. Harvard's decision was applauded by diversity supporters and seen as "wokeness" rhetoric to be weaponized against the left.

Again, the question is, "How did this particular decision [related to something someone said or did to another person who self-identifies as being part of a subordinated group] help everyone grow to greater understanding about inclusive behavior and leadership with an inclusive mindset?"

My response is, "It didn't." In fact, it placed the responsibility on another university or solely back on the shoulders of an eighteen-year-old who has likely never had a dialogue about the impact of his voice. Was there inquiry on where the usage of that type of language originates from? Additionally, if not Harvard, where will he or others who behaved like him end up in college?

Who accepts this student whose exposure after the tragedy (and he is not alone here) may have given him access to networks that helped him get into Harvard? Conversely, it doesn't matter how he got accepted—he did. And rescinding his acceptance without him having the opportunity to engage in dialogue that could be transformative isn't helpful to anyone. As Monica Hesse asks, "So, what should we do with the Kyle Kashuvs of this world?"[13] Of course, Kashuv is not excused for what he said. There are implications for such words, and more so when you've invited the spotlight onto yourself. At the same time, there is a process of redemption that is not only about people like Kashuv. And when I say like Kashuv, I mean any person who has had something they said or did in the past, maybe once or twice, define them forever. And, as a result, all of what they have positively contributed to the world is, for all intents and purposes, canceled.

What the Kyle Kashuvs, the #MeToo-profiled Black males, subjugated Indigenous people, and so on rarely enter into with the so-called "other" is "a zone of productive disequilibrium, a place where we allow enough discomfort to foster productive reflection and change but not so much that people shut down and feel defensive."[14] The complexity of situations requires that these zones are made standard. Organizations should be designed for and educated to make such spaces part of their systems. Zones of productive disequilibrium are designed to be inclusive.

Human beings have always been part of a complex web of mutual influence. For many who never considered this possibility, the impact of COVID-19 provided a window, if not a mirror, to reveal this reality. While some resist this notion and feel like their action and choices are sovereign, this thinking is incomplete. Connectedness is increasing and inevitable; thus, complexity is inevitable. The ever-expanding connectivity and reflective connectedness make systems thinking and inclusion go hand in hand, with urgency.

AI-DEI Humanity Enhanced or Compromised

"The unknown future rolls toward us. I face it, for the first time, with a sense of hope. Because if a machine, a Terminator, can learn the value of human life, maybe we can too."
—**Sarah Connor, Protagonist,** *Terminator 2: Judgment Day*

Causality and Training Data

The opening quote of this chapter is from the final scene of the second film in the *Terminator* franchise. This franchise is perhaps the one that icon Arnold Schwarzenegger is best known for—his line "Hasta la vista, baby!" might be his most famous. In the films, Sarah Connor, aka the mother of the Resistance, birthed John Connor, the resistance leader who leads an army to save the world from a new society of artificial intelligence (AI) named the Terminator(s).

In the final scene, Connor goes into a monologue just after she has lowered the Terminator, played by Schwarzenegger, into a massive foundry to melt it down at its request via its programming. In the first movie, the Terminator had tried to kill Connor and the father of her child. In the second movie, the AI protects Connor, her son, and humans in general. Connor's message, delivered as she's driving down a dark highway and the movie moves toward the closing credits, was that if an AI could learn to value humanity, humans could choose humanity, too.

Many of our organizational DEI initiatives fail because we fail the Terminator test. Rather than structuring our efforts with the superset of humanity in mind, we design them with particular subsets of humanity in mind instead. This is not to say that particular groups don't need appropriate attention given to their unique circumstances. But if humanity is a superset and particular identities are its subsets, then focusing on a specific subset instead of emphasizing the breadth of humanity could be limiting even for those who are the intended targets of our approaches.

AI holds the potential to broaden our insights about humanity. If used thoughtfully, it can mitigate harm in a variety of processes and systems where built-in historical biases can be examined and reconsidered with code. AI can help change the narrative. Conversely, it can also reinforce historical biases that have created inequities. Inequities such as ageism in hiring, colorism in recognizing faces in crime prevention video surveillance systems, and decisions about approving loans could be and have been found to influence training data sets and coding that reflects unequal treatment intentionally and unintentionally perpetuated over time.

The narrative of artificial intelligence (AI) is a mathematical one, input via code. As Fulbright Fellow and Rhodes Scholar Dr. Joy Buolamwini says, "Whoever codes the system embeds her views. Limited views created limited systems." Buolamwini suggests that coding be done with an inclusive lens. She calls it "InCoding."[1] Her vision is that technology reflects the perspectives and interests of its creators *and* users.

Buolamwini's PhD research at the Massachusetts Institute of Technology (MIT) was advanced facial recognition technology. She calls herself an algorithmic bias researcher and a Poet of Code. Her research with colleagues at the MIT Media Lab found that facial recognition technology is not accurate in its identification of dark faces. The research focused on Amazon's cutting-edge facial recognition program, aptly named Rekognition. Buolamwini concluded that the program exhibits gender and racial bias in gender classification.

Their result was not that the technology was "bad," but rather that there was a possibility of abuse and that more oversight was necessary to prevent misuse and negative consequences. Amazon's response was defensiveness, which, while possibly understandable, was not okay considering the potentially harmful and dehumanizing consequences of its program. For example, what if darker faces are wrongly recognized and result in adverse actions by the police? Imagine what could happen to an innocent person due to algorithmic error.

Amazon refused to submit their AI systems to the national regulatory oversight committee of the National Institute of Standards and Technology (NIST) for testing, claiming to be bias free via internal oversight. A few simple changes could have prevented loads of negative press, including the Netflix documentary *Coded Bias*, featuring Buolamwini. This doesn't mean that Rekognition took a significant hit where its customers were concerned. However, anytime the program is used and a dark-skinned person is implicated, reasonable doubt will persist. The system coders' lack of vigilance didn't just negatively impact Amazon; it indirectly compromised all facial recognition programs. Where was Amazon's DEI leadership on an issue of this magnitude?

"If the code being reused has bias, this bias will be reproduced by whoever uses the code for a new project or research endeavor," Buolamwini added. "Unfortunately, reused code at times reflects the lack of inclusion in the tech space in non-obvious but important ways. Commonly used face detection code works in part by using training sets—a group of example images that are described as human faces. The faces that are chosen for the training set impact what the code recognizes as a face. A lack of diversity in the training set leads to an inability to easily characterize faces that do not fit the normal face derived from the training set."[2]

So, the coding determines the outcomes of how the system detects nuances. These nuances start with machine learning (ML) from training data that are uniformly used across the industry. If the training data are incomplete and the system normalizes a certain skin tone and set of features, inherent bias evolves when identifying non-normalized groups. Strip all names and data labels from the data and ask, would I want any group being biased against? Does it matter what group it is?

At the same time, if there's a possibility of negative biases being built into an AI system by humans for human benefit, then we can also build training data sets that represent a broader humanity. As Sarah Connor said (with my embellishing), "If a machine, a Terminator, can learn the value of human life, [then we humans can teach all machines such humanity]."

Algorithms

Upon first learning about AI-powered approaches to debiasing talent management systems, I was excited. I understood that there were potential dark sides, but I was hopeful that we had discovered a way to reduce inequity that was measurable and could be thoughtfully executed.

My excitement led me to share my sentiments with the head of HR of a large Fortune 500 healthcare company. His response was lukewarm. He told me, "Yeah, we will see." Why didn't he engage with me? In truth, I don't know. It's possible that, for him, HR systems were working well. He was successful in his role. His engagement with senior leadership peers was well managed. Perhaps introducing tools that created a different level of accountability and required letting go of a certain amount of control didn't seem appealing. He was one of the key drivers of the current algorithm related to talent at the most senior levels of the organization.

Algorithms have driven our lives far before the rise of artificial intelligence. In fact, our experiences are like the training data set that (mostly unconsciously) drives our individual and organizational behaviors. In our professions, experiences we have had across time lay the foundation for our heuristic strategies—those gut feelings that help us cut through data ambiguity and drive many of our decisions. In short, there's often an equation underneath our intuition.

Machines learn based on instructions we give them and the data they interact with, not experientially. Again, these data inputs and learning materials are selected by humans, similar to the way children learn directly and indirectly from their parents and environments. As Buolamwini says, coders embed their views and values into the instructions they give. Algorithms can reflect the intentions and aspirations of the programmer and all those who are influencing the programmer. Not one person, idea, and belief, but multitudes.

Much of the average person's experience with algorithms comes from the social media platforms they engage with. Many people have decided to quit Meta; some after the FBI investigation's revelations into potential interference in the 2016 US presidential campaign, and others before. Meta's algorithm interacting with specific content exerted an outsized influence on Meta users, therefore very likely unduly influencing the 2016 elections. My rationale for departing from the platform was that the echo chamber that I found myself in while foraging through Meta, and eventually Twitter, felt opposite to the plurality I was interested in. I felt trapped in a loop of the familiar, even when I thought I was intentionally seeking out something "other" to be influenced by. As author and neuroscientist Sam Harris says, "We are all in some sort of echo chamber."

This lack of transparency and inclusion may have led to the 66 percent decline in trust that Meta experienced as a result of reports about the election findings.[3] The Ponemon Institute, an independent research firm specializing in privacy and data protection, indicated that although Meta may not experience immediate declines in its membership, the lack of trust indicates that some users will leave the platform altogether while others will give considerably less of their data and content-sharing time. Not considering inclusion when you have asked people to trust you with how their data are shared seems like something that could be easily prevented.

For companies whose business models depend to any degree on AI (and that pretty much means all companies given how ubiquitous it is), there is a cost that must be paid if keeping customers and talent is important. It is the COST of inclusion. That is Care, Openness, Safety, and Trust.

Care means acknowledging the interdependence of the algorithms, their makers, and their consumers. If the algorithms create something that allows those they are made for to thrive, yet care is absent in that process, the inevitable result is that harm will be done to some extent. If companies expect people to keep openly consenting to giving them their data to train AI on, they must care that the machines can do things that humans cannot. That is, machines are agnostic to the identities of those they are programmed to assess, and the human who wrote their code and the training data used is not. To care is to test the behavior of the algorithms rigorously.

Openness means that if an algorithm is created, it is mandatory for the makers and owners of the ever-evolving code to properly test it and ask questions like, "How would the screening rule's decisions have been different if a particular feature (or features) of the applicant were changed?" Everyday human biases are difficult to detect, particularly over a short time period, not to mention over longer periods. Asking humans to accurately calculate what would change if the breadth of human features were considered in their talent-related decision-making is nearly impossible. In this case, openness means asking specific questions and being transparent about what is being discovered through testing algorithms, reflecting an unambiguous investment that creates the greatest possibility for AI/ML to be a catalyst for good.

Safety as it relates to algorithmic systems requires protecting the interests of those who have opted into or have been processed into a human-machine interaction with an algorithm(s) acting as arbiter between them and a third party (e.g., potential or current employer, financial institution). Most organizations who manufacture goods, do high-tech research and development, and repair items large (power lines and large machinery) and small (electronic devices) have a motto of "safety first." Given the potential for significant harm to those engaged with algorithms, companies must adopt a priority of safety for their digital assets.

This brings us to the last and perhaps most critical element organizations need to consider in their usage and creation of digital assets and their respective algorithms: *Trust.*

Trust from Meta users didn't diminish by nearly 70 percent because their algorithm wasn't working well. The reality of the Meta algorithmic system was that it was working extremely well. Its revenues grew 500 percent from 2015 to 2020.

Meta was moderately transparent, and ironically, that is the problem. They asked for users to allow more access to how their data are used. The trust breach came when they weren't open about why they wanted more access. They didn't explain how this would create greater safety and security for users, which was one of the most critical features and reasons why people preferred WhatsApp.

There is a COST of inclusion. It comes from creating the conditions for people to feel like and perhaps even unambiguously know (as much as this is feasible) that their well-being is prioritized by tech (all) companies; that they care; and that they are open with you because they want to ensure with full trust that you are safe as employees, vendors, or consumers of their products.

In his ethnographical work looking at algorithmic systems, anthropologist Nick Seaver suggests that the issues don't lie in the biases of an individual. Seaver's observations suggest that the popular view of algorithms isn't congruent with the actual practices in how they are created and evolve and by whom they are created. The "makers" of algorithms would not call themselves as such because the piece(s) of code they wrote would be, as a rule, changed by the next person who interacted with it. The final result(s) are multiple algorithms in motion, designed by multiple actors, often without direct connection. Even when they do have direct and regular access, it may not mean much. Given the speed of projects and the volume of work they do, sense-making about code written fifteen months ago is not very likely or very productive.

So, algorithmic systems are interdependent works of collective authorship by design. They are made, maintained, and revised by many people with different goals at different times. And once these systems reach a certain level of complexity, their outputs can be difficult to predict precisely, even for those with technical know-how. Simply making the system transparent does not resolve this basic knowledge problem, which afflicts even "insiders."

Without built-in evaluation systems, the fear of algorithms making the machines turn on humans (à la *Terminator* or the inevitable job losses due to technological advances of AI) is real. In theory, algorithms could produce a cataclysmic event, just like in the *Terminator* franchise.

It's more likely that algorithms, with limited or low-frequency feedback loops, will create oppressive results. Results like past Google results (prior to the company updating its algorithm) when people typed "Black Girls" into the search engine and got pornographic content leading the results.[4] This is indeed a negative result, and one a tad more likely than a large former top bodybuilder showing up to kill his adversary before he was born.[5] And perhaps it's a bit more possible than machines using humans as living batteries to power a digital world, à la *The Matrix*.

The problems of search engines being unknowingly biased toward stereotyping or facial recognition systems that don't correctly assess darker-skinned faces can feel more personal. And biased algorithms exist everywhere. The nature of multiple inputs (multiple observers in a sense) expressly indicates that their inputs and observations change the system. In doing so, their biases become part of the collective similarities and differences in what is often a pool of people contributing to a particular algorithm.

Who Is Telling You What You Like?

When Amazon started suggesting books to me back in the early 2000s, it felt like they sent me an unending gift. My reading list included organizational culture, innovation, and related subjects (i.e., leadership, design, knowledge transfer, social psychology, cultural intelligence, complexity, change, strategy, and more). Amazon pointed me in the right direction, and its recommendations algorithm has consistently evolved.[6] My experience (and that of many others) on other platforms, such as Twitter and Meta, has been different over the same period. The content that I was being fed seemed to be aimed at getting me to take a position or reinforce one that was discerned because I followed a thread of content that took a particular interest in something or a fixed stance on an issue.

In the case of Twitter, its switch to curated timelines after a long-standing approach to chronological ones caught a lot of criticism. They eventually switched back to the chronological approach while keeping the option to see the most popular or trending tweets.[7]

Many users were ecstatic. Other experts felt that people's fear of missing out was a reason why the algorithmic chronology was worthwhile. When the changes happened, Twitter usage went up. Now, one can select settings for a more user-driven, chronological feed, making Twitter the perceived go-to platform for more neutral content. That doesn't make Twitter neutral, and no other social media, machine, or human-driven system is bias free.

We still have to ask ourselves, "Who is telling me what I (should) like?" Of course, some of us have liked the same things for a long time. It's hard to know the origin of our choices and preferences as we've been influenced by our closest analog connections (like friends and family members) over time and by our electronic ones more recently.

We tend to take what is most quickly presented as familiar. For example, consider the predictive text feature on most smartphones. You start to type, and a suggestion for what you should say comes up. In some cases, these suggestions, if enabled, allow you to be pointed to popular language on the web and social media. This is fine, but it also drives us toward sameness. It feeds us things that allow us to have a common preference for a certain lexicon.

One impact is that you are presented with language that resonates and that you incorporate into your lexicon. When you are posting on social media, using certain phrases and idioms, it is being reinforced as the language of your in-group. It is like a feedback loop: Language suggestions → Incorporated into personal lexicon → Lexicon is used in social media → Other people using the lexicon follow and connect, effectively reinforcing their discovery of what they prefer.

We all do this, and it's similar to finding our in-group. DEI people are great at it! We have our own language, inaccessible to most, but each day we try to make it more mainstream by incorporating popular language that is "celebrified" and is desirable by a mass audience. This makes DEI a bit cooler, trendier, more aware of social issues than others. And perhaps a bit more conversation-worthy, especially when topics of mental health, celebrity social justice causes, and identity activism often focused on celebrities are discussed as they are included in the DEI bucket.

The problem is that echo chambers are exclusive. Only certain ideas and people get to enter; most of the time, we let in that with which we are familiar. It is a common trap for DEI practitioners. We too easily attach to particular ideas which can compromise our ear for dissent. DEI practitioners need to be beacons for dissenters. Our responsibility is to home in on the quietest (or even silenced) voices and the loudest resistance. Part of our reason for being is to understand the sentiments, contributions, and insights that come from all areas of the organization.

AI creates many possibilities for inclusion. We can focus on what isn't working or understand the systems in the digital world and take action to establish what works. Humans and AI go hand in hand. And while some believe the technology will eventually outsmart humanity, I am voting for humans predominantly choosing humanity, sustainability, and civility as our long-term modus operandi (with the assistance of AI built with Caring, Openness, Safety, and Trust).

DEI Practitioners: What's Going On?

"Diversity is inherently neither good nor bad, but rather a reality. Its potential for good or bad depends on the particulars of a given situation, the nature of the diversity in question and the capability of individuals to make quality decisions in the midst of differences, similarities, and tension."

—Dr. R. Roosevelt Thomas

Before June 2020, I had never marched in the name of justice. My life in the US had left me numb regarding race. Participating in protests seemed like a waste of time. I appreciated those who marched, impassioned to take a stand for what they felt was right. For me, though, marching for something related to identity didn't translate beyond the symbolic. I felt my time was better spent working and contributing to the places where I could influence change at scale. That is, inside the organizations and institutions where I worked, had access, and carried influence.

The global response to the lynching of George Floyd was different. It pulled me to the streets of Basel. My stepkids and my wife were moved to greater action by this energy. During a global pandemic, against my epidemiological sensibilities, my family was convincing enough that I went out to be a part of the spark. I was moved by the energy of the Swiss teens and twenty-somethings, people of color (mostly Black folks) who organized the event, sharing their stories and calling for solidarity.

The voices of protesters around the world were heard. Many of the organizations listening were compelled to action. In most cases the actions revolved around bringing in speakers to talk about race and racism. The intentions were to be applauded.

More than a year later, the questions that have come up for me are: How broadly influential and impactful have these efforts been? What has the racial justice push created to help all employees (at all levels) see how the work of DEI impacts everyone? The answers naturally vary. I am very confident that seeing the video of a man murdered on your electronic devices is shocking and calls for a dramatic reaction to such inhumanity. I am less confident that it compels people and organizations to elevate the call to action to one that goes beyond focusing on a single dimension of identity.

Today, it seems that every group of inherently diverse constituents is fighting for their relevance and positioning both in society and at the companies where they work. Many use social vehicles, social media, and more to fight for that relevance. The battle for satisfactory identity relevance of inherently diverse groups isn't new, and it's hard to know if it can ever be a battle that can be won.

What do I mean by the inherently diverse? In 2013, the Center for Talent Innovation (CTI, and now Coqual) concluded that "employees at companies with two-dimensional (2D) diversity are more likely than employees at non-diverse companies to take risks, challenge the status quo, and embrace a diverse array of inputs." Two-dimensional diversity is defined as leadership that has three or more types of each of the two categories of diversity.

- *Inherent diversity:* gender, race, age, religious background, socio-economic background, sexual orientation, disability, nationality
- *Acquired diversity:* cultural fluency, generational savvy, gender [literacy], social media skills, cross-functional knowledge, global mindset, military experience, language skills[1]

CTI's research concluded that 22 percent of companies in its representative sample had 2D diversity. Furthermore, those that had it were 70 percent more likely to capture a new market.

Often referred to as the "father of diversity," the late Dr. Roosevelt Thomas defined diversity in a broader fashion than CTI, as his emphasis was on successfully and sustainably managing diversity. The foundation of multiple distinctions beyond race and gender was similar. He defined diversity as "any collective mixture characterized by differences, similarities, and related tensions and complexities."[2]

In his book *Beyond Race and Gender,* Thomas stated, "Managing diversity means approaching diversity at three levels simultaneously: individual, interpersonal, and organizational. The traditional focus has been on individual and interpersonal aspects alone. What is *new* is seeing diversity as an issue for the entire organization, involving the very way organizations are structured."[3]

Thomas wrote about this "new" approach in 1991. Yet, thirty years later, our DEI practices are still stuck on race and gender. In the words of the great Marvin Gaye, "What's Going On?"

I could articulate far too many reasons why DEI is not working, from my experience. First and foremost is the fact that organizations have historically focused a great deal of their resources on so-called talent diversity, which others, including myself, call representation with an emphasis on gender and race. I believe representation matters. So, the efforts could be worthwhile if they were working; however, they are not.

Over the past decade, Frank Dobbin and Alexandra Kalev have researched corporate diversity efforts. They have found some things that work, such as diversity managers, diversity task forces, and mentoring—as well as many things that do not work, including mandatory diversity training, diversity scorecards, and managerial engagement. Dobbin and Kalev indicated that some of these, especially mandatory diversity training, not only failed to make an impact on representation numbers but also hindered inclusion and could impair existing efforts. Conversely, companies making training available and voluntary saw some increases in managerial representation diversity. [4]

When Dobbin and Kalev first started publishing their research about what was and wasn't working in the DEI world, especially around the effectiveness of DEI training, the resistance was abundant. At the time, like many pioneering diversity firms and solo practitioners around the US (many of which were focused on diversity training), I pretty much dismissed their work. Several years later, as I began to get back to my research orientation— that is, one that asked unbiased questions—I found research and spoke with some academic and applied researchers that agreed with Dobbin and Kalev's work over the past twelve to thirteen years.

The challenges we face as a field aren't limited to our lack of evidence in popular interventions. Despite studies that have alleged the innovation and financial benefits of diversity—like that of CTI and those of McKinsey & Company for the past several years—we have yet to see sustainable movement toward what we can uniformly identify as "progress."[5] Our primary challenge isn't that many US-centric diversity interventions and research efforts have been carried out in "single-nation settings, which is insufficient for the complexities that multinational corporations are dealing with." Our problem is one of a selectively narrowed scope.

DEI Has Been Reduced

With the lack of "success" of diversity programs, the efficacy institutions' DEI work faces increased scrutiny. Many companies respond by doing more of what is not working.

As the push for efforts around racial justice and anti-racism have reemerged as a priority, firms have once again had to react to current events and sentiments. George Floyd's murder-by-asphyxiation left people with a range of emotions, from disbelief to traumatic confirmation. Through viewing Floyd's dehumanizing death, the world was given a glimpse of what many Black people experience in different ways.

Of course we, as in the world and the places where people are employed, had to respond. There was a calling for us to be deliberate in challenging the history of brutality that has been perpetuated toward darker-skinned people who are part of the African diaspora. The need to do so has always been with us. What we have never had on a global stage is the space to openly talk about race and racial injustice inside of organizational life. Floyd's tragic death created a window of opportunity for something transformational to emerge.

That is not what has happened. Rather than the opportunity for truth and reconciliation, we have created a "my truth and why you should pay me for telling it to you" dynamic. Since June of 2020, we have seen the emergence of more DEI, racial justice, and anti-racism "experts" than perhaps we will ever see again. People have been using their "lived experience" to build personal brands with the intention of transformation. It is hard to understand what qualifies many of these emergent experts to lead organizations through the complexity that the confluence of a global pandemic, peaking racial tension, and political extremism have made more visible. Yet, their push for racial justice has been received, and many firms have welcomed them openly to educate and be in dialogue with their employees.

My optimism and belief that most people are well meaning leads me to conclude that most people who entered the DEI space in 2020 did so with a passion to make change. And while the financial incentives that go along with such entry are evident, I will hold that as a secondary or tertiary motivation. Nonetheless, the willingness and passion to lead people toward creating sustainable shifts in an organizational culture is insufficient. A single-minded focus on race can lead to people thinking of this single attribute as a monolithic notion.

DEI practitioners have done this for a long time, even prior to George Floyd. If their focus is on empowering women, their lens is on increasing agency for women. The LGBTQA+ community focuses on its own self-advocacy and policy. Latinos, Asians (without distinction), Native Americans, those with disabilities, and others present their respective needs to the organizations they belong to. This has been the way for such a long time that we think it is the only way we can move things forward for these respective groups and the organizations where they make their contributions. The problem is that there is little to no evidence that reducing people to single attributes of their identities leads organizations to creating the conditions for everyone to thrive. In fact, the problem might be that we spend a great deal of time focusing on people's identities as problems. The reality is that DEI, if practiced in a more expansive and less reductionist manner, can create unlimited space and possibilities for cultural transformation.

There isn't a single answer to the DEI "problems" that we are facing. DEI is an idea to be explored and iterated on, not a "problem" to be solved. If we looked at all the things that DEI programs take on, we'd find they consist of advocating for many humankinds. And the approaches address a long list of inter/intrapersonal and organizational dynamics that have existed since humans, carrying their respective distinctions, have assembled.

The narrative of many DEI practitioners doesn't reflect what Dr. Roosevelt Thomas stated about managing diversity—that it requires "a comprehensive managerial process for developing an environment that works for all employees." Rather, too much of the work has focused on pointing out how particular groups have been negatively impacted by what is blanketly framed as systemic racism. This has led to a confirmatory search for evidence (lived experiences) to back up such claims. Once the search for what is racist, sexist, homo/transphobic, and/or wrong is embarked upon, it is usually discovered. This doesn't mean that the discovered personal examples aren't worthy of being addressed for everyone's benefit. It also doesn't mean that surfacing such stories reveals an organization to be inherently or overwhelmingly filled with toxicity. It just means that our focus, while good-hearted, is overly simplistic and narrow.

I don't see progress in this paradigm. Judging from conversations with other practitioners, many of us are on the same page. Nonetheless, the reductionist stance persists. Why can't we stop reducing people to single attributes of their identity and start elevating who they are and what they bring to organizational life?

Respecting Perseverance

When thinking about the DEI field and all the hard and very emotionally taxing work that has been contributed over the years to corporate social justice, I am often reminded of a *Sesame Street* skit that I watched as a child. Jim Henson was the voice of the puppet Henry, and Academy Award–winning Actress Rita Moreno was Liza, Henry's wife. They sang a song about a *deadlock situation*. If you haven't seen the video, it is an easy DuckDuckGo search away. Imagine the rising frustration of Liza as the song progresses. The lyrics start off with Henry telling Liza about his problem of a hole (in his bucket). Liza responds that he should fix it, and the result is that with all of Liza's suggestions, Henry has a counterpoint ending exactly where he began; there is still a hole in the bucket because none of what was suggested could be done without having an intact container from the outset.

If you watch the video, Liza reaches a point of no return. She goes silent and resigns, ceasing her desire to play in what turns out to be a deadlocked exchange.

So, the problem with DEI is not the problem. There is a hole in the bucket and our conversational networks of contention keep us deadlocked in an exchange that is full of conflict. But as a field we have rarely sought out common frameworks to resolve them.

We have tried to make shifts with language. We have introduced and reintroduced language and phenomena from various sociological and psychological theories. Terms like "equity," "belonging," and phenomena such as "psychological safety" and "cognitive/unconscious bias" have been put forward as explanations for what's not working, aspirations for the work, and things to do to get there (e.g., debiasing or mitigating unconscious bias, focusing on people feeling as though they belong and don't have to "cover"). We have moved from diversity management through diversity and inclusion; inclusion and culture; inclusion and belonging; equity and inclusion; and, most recently, DEI. Some very experienced practitioners have even created a set of Global Diversity, Equity, and Inclusion Benchmarks (GDEIB). More recently, the International Organization for Standardization (ISO) has created an international guidance on diversity and inclusion.[6] Our perseverance and persistence toward evolving the work of DEI is impressive and something I am deeply appreciative and respectful of.

Most of these shifts in the field have been the result of a few people, though—leading voices in the forms of a larger consultancy or an influential personality in the space. We have created very few clear frameworks that can be examined over longer periods of time and to come to conclusions about what can work, when, and where. Meaning, we have started using language and approaches with hope, but not with evidence. There are quite a few stories told about some of the introduced approaches that have worked for a few organizations, but there's not much data showing that such interventions worked across many organizations over multiple years.

As practitioners, we have not consistently or generally been clear with the organizations with whom we work about DEI outcomes that bring value for all stakeholders. I believe clarity on outcomes is a must. "Best practices," for instance, should be articulated as "(best) practices for organizations currently experiencing _____" or "(best) practices for organizations aspiring to create _____" (fill in the blanks). For me, the outcomes of DEI always include people (all stakeholders) thriving and a generative organizational culture thriving. Both can be measured with clarity. The pathways, activities, learning, and policies to achieve these outcomes are many.

The Middle Path

We have set DEI efforts in motion via civil rights activism, social justice, humanitarian, social, and moral responsibility that led many to engage in DEI careers. These are all legitimate, and to abandon them would be draining to the historical spirit of DEI. When thinking about the summary of our social justice efforts and desire for our organizations to be good corporate citizens, once again, Dr. Roosevelt Thomas asks an incisive question: "What do the best interests of society dictate that we should do?"[7] And, I would add: Whom should we be doing it for?

The answer to that last question is *everyone*.

I have always been fascinated with labyrinths. I love the complexity of their designs, the sacred geometry, the contextual elegance of their designer(s), and, more uniformly, the structure and purpose of labyrinths.

Unlike mazes, labyrinths have one way in and out of their ending point. They have a single possibility for those who enter to reach the ultimate destination, which lies in the center.

All must enter with the intention of reaching this center point. This center point is not a destination where, once reached, one wins. Rather, it is a destination toward a new beginning. A point that, upon entering, we reflect, we ponder and convey to all who have taken the journey and all who follow what we learned with each turn, each impasse, each step.

As a DEI field, it is time we escape from the conversational networks of contention, the cycles of reincarnation, the cautionary brand, the deadlocks. Our days of pursuing mostly incomplete ideas and ideals, and of not evolving personally or organizationally, need to end. There is a calling to the extraordinary, a calling that spoke for most of us when we began this work, that we need to return to.

This calling to the extraordinary asks us to thoughtfully enter the complexity of the labyrinth we have created. It is a calling that is agnostic to everything (existing beyond our attachments, preferences, traditions, and desires for the elevation of a single idea or identity) and that chooses only humanity. Entering this labyrinth won't be without frustration. It won't eradicate conflict. There will be turns that we learn from and turns that leave us saddened and angry. Nonetheless, the center of the labyrinth will serve as a space for all of us, which is the true nature of belonging, equity, and inclusion.

Up to now, I have walked the path of purposeful deconstruction of DEI, mindfully pulling apart various aspects of DEI because to find that center we must first understand what's preventing us from seeing it or reaching it.

I'll start the second part of this book by reconstructing these elements into what I call an *Inclusion System*. The process of deconstruction and reconstruction will continue in part throughout the rest of this book. My aim in shaping the idea of an Inclusion System isn't for it to be definitive or static, but dynamic and emergent. It is an entry point—from wherever we may take our first steps on the journey of continuous refinement—moving toward the center of the labyrinth.

I hope you will join me on this path.

Part
Two

Reconstructing:
The Inclusion System

"Every system is perfectly designed to get the results it gets."
—W. Edwards Deming

In the winter of 2019, my stepson Rafael began to watch his friend Moritz juggle. At some point after watching Moritz for a while, Rafael tried to juggle. Like most people trying something for the first time, he didn't find immediate success. Rafael was looking at the entirety of the task and wanting to jump to the outcome that he saw when watching Moritz.

Moritz showed Rafael how to juggle using two "props" (i.e., rubber balls) with the shower method and one hand. Rafael began to pick up on the one-handed technique. The next day, Moritz had him use two hands with two balls using the cascade pattern. Soon thereafter, Rafael moved to three balls. Within a month, he began teaching me and his sister (she was less interested), and then the kids in the neighborhood. I imagine when his little brother is old enough and amply coordinated, he will instruct him, too.

Moritz took Rafael through an inductive process. Juggling is complex, but when broken down into its component parts, the complexity is mitigated. In our respective businesses, we are juggling every day. We are not only juggling business priorities, but also all the other "props" we choose in life. Former Coca-Cola CEO Brian Dyson once gave a speech about work-life balance where he said, "Imagine life as a game in which you are juggling some five balls in the air. You name them—work, family, health, friends, and spirit—and you're keeping all of these in the air. You will soon understand that work is a rubber ball. If you drop it, it will bounce back. But the other four balls—family, health, friends, and spirit—are made of glass. If you drop one of these, they will be irrevocably scuffed, marked, nicked, damaged or even shattered. They will never be the same. You must understand that and strive for balance in your life."[1]

I've heard many executives use this juggling analogy from the former Fortune 100 CEO when describing how they seek to maintain a healthy life and work integration. Priorities are given to those things most critical to long-term success. Imagine organizations that use such an analogy. Less likely, perhaps, they encourage similar categories explicitly. Conversely, let's assume that a firm's glass and rubber props are about what we might label as business priorities (or systems if you may). That is, strategy, customers, talent development, innovation, lowering costs, and increasing profitability.

One could say, "These balls don't seem to have 'inclusion' among them, so what is your point?" Inclusion isn't a ball in the act of juggling. *Inclusion*, in terms of an organization, *is the act of juggling itself.* Adjusting to accommodate the variation in the organization, knowing the complexity of each prop on its own, and at times being required to add props and various things needing to be balanced. Inclusion, when in action, is the system of keeping things in the air and sometimes knowing which things will bounce back and which things need to be temporarily placed on the table so that the right attention can be given to the other elements without irreparable consequences.

If inclusion were a ball, it would be great if companies included it as a priority. However, the complexity and necessity of it doesn't allow for it to be prioritized as such. It must be a system integrated with other systems. A system that consistently touches all the other systems; that interacts with them, observes how they interact, and informs them in a manner that allows for each to be better than it was via their myriad interactions and growing interdependency.

The first sections of this book were dedicated to mindfully deconstructing the concepts and thinking that have brought us to where we currently are in the DEI space. We will now pivot toward what we are trying to create, or reconstruct, if you may.

In this starting point to the book's second section, I will reconstruct the inclusion paradigm. I'll begin with a description of what reconstruction means in this context. From there, we will move through the necessary elements to designing an Inclusion System. The remaining chapters will describe these elements (also known as requirements in the language of classical systems development architecture) and their importance in creating and perpetually refining your Inclusion System.

All organizations function via their systems. Whether those systems are related to tangibles, like their supply chain and manufacturing, or intangibles, like sales or recruitment systems, when these schemes don't operate well, businesses suffer. Conversely, when they are optimized, organizations thrive.

Management scholar W. Edwards Deming said, "It would be better if everyone worked together as a system, with the aim for everybody to win."[2] In designing an Inclusion System, the intention is to construct your inclusion paradigm so that everyone can win. I like to say, "When inclusion wins, everyone wins." It is why I advocate for inclusiveness to be accessible, actionable, and sustainable. It must be viewed and designed systemically.

An Inclusion System is a vector in the development of a complex adaptive system. We can think about a vector in the sense of physics or epidemiology. If we take the example of physics, an Inclusion System in an organization will provide direction and momentum for complex adaptive systems. As the world has been introduced and overwhelmed with epidemiology and/or epidemiologists since the coronavirus pandemic, I will use such an example as well. In an epidemiological model, an Inclusion System would serve as a host for inclusive actions and habits—a vehicle to transfer inclusive skills, practices, policies, and behaviors throughout an organization.

Organizations of all sizes qualify as complex adaptive systems. Levels of complexity differ from firm to firm and generally correlate with degrees and dimensions of diversity. Given the constant state of market flux, they seek to find ways to go from change and disruption to a state of familiar equilibrium. Organizations and the individuals who are part of them seek to return to such equilibrium even when it won't seemingly benefit them, at least not in the long term.

An Inclusion System as a vector (keeping with the epidemiological metaphor) sits between change and equilibrium, or resistance to change. In one sense, it seeks to induce and inspire change with individuals, groups, and their environments. Simultaneously, it is managing the tension created by the introduction of change or disruption. We have seen this practiced by public health and government officials during the coronavirus pandemic. The virus brought mass and inevitable change. People have sought to resist the disruption physically, socially, and economically. Those working with the public sought to understand the biological components while accounting for anticipated and unknown stressors of the public.

One could say that a robustly designed Inclusion System can contribute to making organizations what Nassim Taleb has coined as *antifragile*—leaning into and engaging with resistance, stressors, disruptions, and disequilibrium and catapulting forward because of such engagement.[3]

Reconstructing inclusion is meant to be similar to social reconstruction. Social reconstruction seeks to create the conditions where populations, or in our case organizations, can facilitate an ongoing practice of truth telling through which a community or society moves from a divided past toward the co-creation of a peaceful coexistence in a shared future.

My objective is to create a space to speak truth and examine context in DEI. That means creating a path forward for everyone to recognize the benefits of inclusion individually and collectively. Reconstructing in this sense is about creating organizational systems and networks where everyone belongs. In such systems and networks, robust social capital is created encouraging people to grow with one another in times when organizations are at ease. And more so in much of the time when volatility, uncertainty, complexity, and ambiguity are at play.

Before going into details about what an Inclusion System is and what it does, let's start with a couple of definitions:

- **Diversity:** Any mixture of similar and different attributes and their respective tension and complexities.[4]
- **Equity:** *Vigilantly* identifying where fairness, context, or access gaps exist—generatively *learning and designing* what's needed to close them.
- **Inclusion:** (*verb*) Actions that create the conditions for any mixture of similar and different attributes to thrive and for an organization to be generative.

Inclusion is a relational construct, meaning that the conditions created via actions taken are meant to deepen individual and organizational capacity to better relate with all stakeholders. Any organizational practice, behavior, and systemic or structural change that is intended to help people become more open to sharing and willing to be influenced by people whose backgrounds are less familiar than their own, connotes practicing inclusion.

- **Thrive:** To flourish. Progressing or realizing one's goals despite or due to temporary circumstances.
- **Generative organizational cultures:** Are positive and life-giving. They create and invent opportunities for others while creating value for themselves. They are highly cooperative, connected, and performance oriented.

In the development and design of an Inclusion System, the above definitions are the guideposts and outcomes/outputs of the system. Thriving stakeholders and generative organizational cultures are *always* among the outputs.

Five Foundational Elements of an Inclusion System

These foundational elements may already be a part of your current DEI approach. If so, the evolution of your Inclusion System is on solid footing. If you don't find these elements in your approach, they should be used as a guide.

1—Accessible, Actionable, Sustainable

An Inclusion System assures that inclusion is integrated into an organizational culture in the following ways:

Accessible means that an Inclusion System is *for everyone* in an organization, and everyone is invited to contribute to its design; be open and safely critical of it; or make a case for changing what it needs to do more of, differently, or stop doing. Furthermore, it recognizes that those who initially engage in the formal design will be a fraction of the whole. An Inclusion System intentionally finds channels to move that fraction closer to "1," or completeness.

Actionable means that *inclusion is unambiguously prioritized* in the organization. While it has ever-emerging philosophies and approaches, the ongoing set of actions and behaviors are communicated with clear expectations of all organizational stakeholders without regard to power or position.

Sustainable means that an Inclusion System is *created to fulfill organizational purpose.* An Inclusion System is a helping force for all stakeholders (i.e., employees, shareholders, suppliers, and customers/users of products and services) to thrive and advance the organizational culture to be generative.

Sustainability goes beyond traditional connotations of the term mainly focused on the natural environment. Climate action is in scope, but more important is sustaining and growing social capital to address complex social and business challenges.

2—Interdependence

An Inclusion System acts to foster interdependence. It acts as a system in and of itself but can only operate interdependently engaged with other organizational systems. An Inclusion System functions as a system within a system.

3—Mindful Reflection

An Inclusion System reflects on itself constantly. In maintaining its insightfulness, it must be measured and challenged for integrity and viability. An Inclusion System uses the behavioral and social sciences as tools for measuring, evaluating, learning, and telling stories about the impact of its co-creations with other systems. Measures can vary. There can be measures of the inputs to evaluate the uptake and resonance. Most important, however, are the measures of the outcomes and impact.

4—Skilled Operators

An Inclusion System requires skilled system operators. There are many people in organizations that consider themselves DEI practitioners. Some have adjacent skills that transcend traditional DEI experience. Others are passionate about the work based on their lived experiences. Skill levels will vary.

Skilled operators are like Moritz, who taught my stepson Rafael how to juggle. They help people to constantly build capabilities so that more skilled operators are available to the organization.

To a lesser extent, Inclusion Systems require the rhetorically gifted to champion and communicate intentions, actions, and outcomes. Operator skill should outweigh rhetorical skills at least 2:1. All organizations should aspire to diligently growing the skilled operator to rhetorically gifted ratio. Showing is greater than telling.

5—Adherence to Core Elements

The core elements of an emerging Inclusion System are like a mirror for the inputs selected. If any input of the system is found to be out of alignment with the core elements and doesn't create the conditions for the above in the fulfillment of its mission, it should be discontinued.

It is possible to assess the prevalence of the foundational elements qualitatively or quantitatively. Such an assessment can be made simple with the following questions associated with each of the five elements. These questions can be utilized either during the inclusive system development phase, or as a stand-alone. You can ask them qualitatively in dialogue or qualitatively to selected stakeholders using a Likert scale.

1. **Accessible, Actionable, Sustainable:** To what extent are our DEI approaches broadly co-created and consistently assessed for whether they are meeting both the needs of all stakeholders and the organizational mission?

2. **Interdependence (with organizational systems):** Where in the organization is inclusion being considered in organizational strategy? How is inclusion being integrated into team engagement and performance metrics? What systems in your organizational design are explicitly considering inclusion in their operation?

3. **Mindful Reflection:** How frequently do you engage with stakeholders as to how inclusion supports them individually, their teams, and the organization in pursuit of its purpose/mission?

4. **Skilled Operators:** In what ways are you assuring that your practitioner community is growing its capability to make inclusion accessible, actionable, and sustainable? How are you actively working to build skills and abilities for emerging operators (e.g., Employee Resource Group, or ERG, members, DEI council and committee members, team leaders)?

5. **Adherence to Core Elements:** What does your data tell you about the impact of your programmatic efforts? Are there regular conversations about how inclusion-oriented programming (explicitly stated to be intended for this purpose) or adjacent efforts (having elements that could be inclusion-oriented) are meeting or exceeding expectations or not? Is the sustainability of these efforts in consideration?

Process and Principles in Developing
an Inclusion System

Systems engineers across many industries use a standard approach to developing systems. This process for technical and non-technical is called the systems development life cycle (SDLC). We will use it as our guide in describing how we create an Inclusion System. The phases are: 1. Analysis; 2. Requirements (Vision of future state); 3. Design / Design Thinking; 4. Development; and 5. Implementation (Refinement).[5]

The SDLC is iterative. It remains in motion, shifting to meet organizational needs as they emerge. An Inclusion System does the same.

Following the SDLC steps informs the steps to be taken as one creates, evolves, or reconstructs an Inclusion System. What to keep in mind is that many organizations have something similar to an Inclusion System. They have various components, and their DEI work may even reflect some of the core principles. What is more likely is that they have developed their approaches in a manner that started with various parts without explicitly intending them to cohesively function. It is also likely that engagement with various organizational systems has been inconsistent, primarily related to the talent acquisition system to debias recruitment and increase representation of historically overlooked, underexposed, and marginalized groups.

Now we will move through the development and design of an Inclusion System using the modified phases of SDLC described above.

1. Analysis

Analysis entails inquiry to gain clarity about the current state of the organization.

Most organizations and consulting firms that work in DEI or organizational development use various data sources to assess the organization's current state. Many are sufficient and allow for problems to surface. For the most part, their analysis reveals few surprises. You could even describe much of what emerges "the unthought known." This means that during the analysis phase, your internal team leading the inquiry or an external consultant says things that "might be consistent with participants' actual observations and experiences . . . they are often not thought of in productive ways that positively influence change. In other words, they are frequently unconscious and taken for granted."[6]

This familiarity is important. Conversely, some parts of an analysis, depending on the extent, will bring different levels of resistance. For example, since the murder of George Floyd, organizations have been introduced to the idea of racial equity audits. The intention of such analysis is to provide recommendations on observations of internal policies, external communications, and organizational practices as they pertain to goals of racial equity for a company. Such audits can serve as part of the analysis for an organization developing an Inclusion System. And, if the audit centers on problems that influential organizational actors have been blind to, the defensiveness will likely be high. The lack of familiarity (to the unconscious mind) creates the resistance.

If an organization takes on an analysis that they can anticipate will result in heavier than expected resistance, it may be worthwhile to couple it with data that speak to what is familiar. As a practitioner, I broadly inquire into what is making the organization function at its current level and what it will take for it to evolve to levels beyond (e.g., to be a generative organization). And what would you, as an individual, member of a team, leader, customer, or another stakeholder, need to thrive and best contribute to the firm's evolution?

While something like a racial equity audit will find problems that some of the Black people (and other people of color) in the company might expect and allies have also potentially observed, such data might be inaccessible to engage making sense of together. There are systems producing what is being experienced as racism for some. The behaviors, policies, and structures creating how people experience the organization's current state always come in many forms. It is likely that what is experienced as ethnicization to some is occurring as ostracism, ageism, favoritism, or some other form of toxicity to others.

The analysis phase of Inclusion System development is meant to help people understand organizational context. This means that people make sense of it together, understanding what is working and what is not and for whom. As you create your Inclusion System, the dialogue will serve as the entry point to creating the inputs (actions) that will create systemic and sustainable change over time.

2. Requirements

What does a generative organization where everyone can thrive look like? How does it feel? What are the everyday things people can do to bring this envisioned future into reality?

When we think about requirements, we first want to consider questions like these that allow us to dream about, envision, and co-create the future state in words. There is a saying often attributed to philosopher Ludwig Wittgenstein: "Words create worlds." Thus, we must work to bring our future to life in the present using language. The result of robust dialogue, starting with these questions, allows the vision for the future to manifest with a shared lexicon that can serve as a touchstone throughout the change journey.

The requirements as they will be described in the next several chapters are not an exhaustive list. You should, however, consider them complete and adequate to use as requirements in your Inclusion System development and design.

If the core elements are followed, that is, if you are indeed committed to creating an Inclusion System, the requirements described in the next several chapters will be adequate for this purpose. And, while I recommend the inclusion of all the requirements to elevate the diversity maturity[7] of your organization, there are three crucial ones that I see as essential to building an Inclusion System for your organization.

I have placed requirements into three overlapping categories. They include:

1. *Mindset/Unlearning* to rethink and more deeply understand how to choose appropriate action. I discuss and highly recommend sense-making and learning related to othering (chapter seven), meritocracy (chapter eight), intersectionality (chapter nine), and exclusion (chapter ten).

2. *Skill sets* are about going beyond willingness and into building a set of capabilities. The most important skill set I recommend is that of cultural intelligence (chapter twelve), as it consists of a set of skills that evidence reinforces (and I have experienced and observed) that enhance organization-wide capabilities and provide a common lens whereby people can recognize their own cultural values and preferences in relation to others inside and outside of the firm.

3. *Structure and Data* refers to measurements that allow insights beyond representation alone. The chapters on social capital (chapter thirteen) and inclusively aligned organizational design (chapter eleven) fall into this category.

3. Design and Design Thinking

The foundational elements and the three categories of requirements listed above anchor the design of an Inclusion System and will guide chosen inputs.

Design thinking is critical to developing your Inclusion System because it is human-centric. It emphasizes empathy, experimentation, and inclusion through idea generation—it's generative. Through it, you create the greatest possibility to take the requirements and consider how to best deploy them and iteratively make necessary adjustments as you do.

Similar to how a software engineer would do their best to prevent bugs that might occur in the development and implementation phases, in the design phase of inclusion systems development you are considering what can enable robust uptake and application of a requirement. And you are being thoughtful about those bottlenecks you can anticipate and realistic about those that will require a response that you can't possibly know and will need to adapt to as they emerge.

4. Development

This is the development of the Inclusion System that an engineer might call the production or installation stage.

Based on what was learned and discussed through the analysis, requirements, and design phases, we will clarify and confirm the inputs the organization will implement now and in the future, as well as the urgency and priority they are given.

If you do not have employee resource groups or a DEI council or committee, this may be the time to consider developing one, even if it will start as a relatively smaller group. They will take on the role of rhetorically gifted champions and, depending on their experience and expertise, skilled operators. Over time, the idea will be for them to all have a level of DEI maturity and dexterity to play the role of skilled operators.

5. Implementation

This is where you take the development of your inputs and insert them into the system to get feedback.

As you can see in Figure 2, once you commence with an input, the process necessitates that the input leads to capability and skill building. Let's walk through our Inclusion Systems development model with a more concrete example of how the process works.

In pharmaceutical research, every project requires rigorous safety checks from bench to bedside. This means thorough assessment of how toxicity might be affecting a patient in a manner that could be adverse or severe—leading to morbidity and, in fewer cases, mortality.

When first testing a drug, these safety experiments are done with in vitro cells, then in animal models, and eventually in patients. The role of the

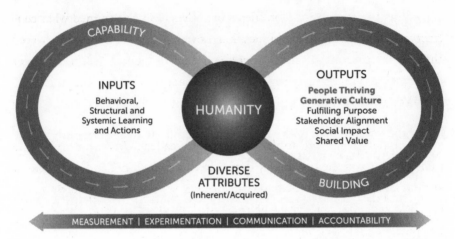

Figure 2

preclinical safety team is critical. However, during testing of an immunology drug by a large pharmaceutical company known for its expertise in developing medicine for immunological conditions, the safety experts deployed on project teams were frustrated that some team members, mainly biologists and chemists, were engaging with them as external service providers.

Members of a preclinical safety team came to me and said, "We feel like we are being left out and underutilized in the project teams."

Their inclusion challenge, or tension if you may, was that they felt like they weren't receiving the kind of respect needed to optimally make contributions to their projects. Although they were listed as team members, they weren't being included as fully embedded members of the drug discovery teams.

We discovered in dialogue that the drug discovery teams considered their role to be confined to safety, making their contribution limited to the part of monthly meetings where safety fell on the agenda. Thus, the teams were not consistently sharing information with them throughout the project so that the safety team could better anticipate needs and give them optimal insight to generate the data they needed to advance their projects.

We conducted a two-hour educational and practice session with the team members and leadership on contracting, which is often used in management consulting to create clarity for clients or colleagues.[8] We framed what contracting can be and had a dialogue about how it could work. We also covered the way the preclinical safety experts could go to their project team leader colleagues and unambiguously say to them what they were going to deliver.

They rehearsed their scripts and then went to the project team leaders across multiple projects.

The safety leads said to the project team leaders, "We want to be able to deliver for you the best safety data, safety information, and engagement around safety possible so that you can advance your project as quickly as you can. We want your project to be successful. And we want to give you the best safety data to get there."

The project team leaders responded, "Absolutely. That's exactly what we want."

The safety leads paused and then said, "To do that, here's what we need from you."

And they made their requests.

Request One: We need to be included in the entirety of the project. Meaning, if you are having additional meetings that are related to the project, we want to be informed, or, even better, invited to those meetings.

Request Two: We want to be able to anticipate what's coming along the way for a project.

"So," the safety leads continued, "if there's something that you're talking about offline, we need to be made aware of that as much as possible. And we want to make sure that all team members know that we're here as advisors and peers to support the project for patients, just like all of us are here for."

After these safety leads did their contracting with team leaders, the project team leaders went to all project team members. "Here's what preclinical safety would like to be able to do," they said. "Here's what they need from you."

Preclinical safety had much better outcomes in terms of working with their project teams following this approach. The safety folks also felt like they were fully included as team members. The project team members outside of preclinical safety conveyed that they were getting more from their safety colleagues, and that projects were moving more smoothly and quickly.

Inclusion became a means for everyone to get what they wanted. They created the outcomes without ever having to call it that. In this example, everyone learned from a relatively simple input. It can be considered an inclusion intervention. At the same time, it was an intervention that was all about the team.

In this case, the input that contributed toward developing an Inclusion System was contracting. In another, it might be behaviors related to creating psychological safety, dignity, mentoring, or virtual meetings education.

Another important element to note is that in Inclusion System development, all inputs, outputs, and the learning loop in between are aimed at elevating humanity. It's critical to make it clear that with any input chosen, humanity must win. That means everyone.

As mentioned earlier, many of the DEI efforts that we see are aiming to address inequity, bias, or injustice as it relates to distinct groups, not connoting humanity. If these inputs are chosen collectively (on the superset, i.e., humanity itself), they are exactly those that the organization should be developing capabilities around. But if a particular input is focused on a single identity or on an element of a particular identity group (a subset of humanity), organizations must clarify how such an input leads to the outcomes or aspirations of an Inclusion System, as we've defined it above: a set of principles and organizationally established requirements, combined with relational practices, that serves as a vehicle to create generative organizations where everyone can thrive and contribute their best.

Remember, like Moritz and Rafael, we are learning to juggle (better) and teach juggling step-by-step. The best way to do this is practice, focusing on refining (or in our case reconstructing) each requirement or input. The other phases will naturally come to fruition as you do.

7

Rooting (for) Them (out)

"The grand prize in us versus them is that somebody gets to feel special for a while. The grand prize in the game of unity is that everyone gets to feel special forever."

—**Deepak Chopra**, *Fire in the Heart*

ob Marley and the Wailers' last album to be released while Marley was alive was *Uprising*. Marley died from cancer less than a year later. During the *Uprising* tour, Marley and the Wailers played before massive crowds while opening for some of the biggest musical stars in the world including Fleetwood Mac and the Commodores. The influence of Bob and his band of brethren was more powerful than ever, drawing record-setting crowds as headliners of more than 120,000.

The song "We and Dem," like many Marley tunes, has a biblical theme referencing Genesis 1:26: "And God said, Let *us* make man in our image, after our likeness: and let *them* have dominion over the fish of the sea, and over the fowl of the air, and over the cattle, and over all the earth" (italics provided by the author for emphasis). He continues referencing Galatians 6:8:

"For he that soweth to his flesh shall of the flesh reap corruption; but he that soweth to the Spirit shall of the Spirit reap life everlasting."

Marley's reference to the flesh was not one pointed at a moral dilemma between meat eaters and non-meat eaters. He intended to describe a mindset. A corrupt mindset that was about power, accumulating material wealth, and sowing hatred, greed, evil, fear, and confusion.

This resonated with the Spirit "overstanding," common terminology in Marley's chosen religion, Rastafarianism. As a Jamaican-born Rastafarian friend of mine described to me in my college days, "Brother Amri, Jah nah want you to understand, you know. Jah want you to overstand. Jah want you to have Jah wisdom and love to overstand Babylon, you know?"

At the time, I nodded my head fervently in agreement, not sure if I did over- or understand. However, after I left his presence, I thought, *Wow, that is a powerful way to look at the world.*

I'm still not sure if I could get away with describing the notion of overstanding as passionately. However, that conversation gave me my first glance into thinking about taking a stand—not as an outward proclamation but rather an inward commitment to something bigger than myself. What is the power of being guided by principles generated from a place deep within? Can this lead to a mindset seeking to transform that which is out of alignment with such principles with light and love, without force?

Marley's lyrics reference a conundrum of sorts. He was a religious/spiritual man guided by a sense of creating art to foster love and goodwill toward humanity. His music had become, by and large, rebellious anthems for the people, especially those who had benefited less from the political and economic systems that predominated the Western world and those colonized by Western nation-states. He also was adamant (as far back as 1976 when politicians were trying to claim his support) about doing all he could to maintain a sort of political neutrality. In 1976, Bob wrote one of his most popular songs, "One Love."[1]

This almost cost him his life. His neutrality led a free concert for unity of all Jamaicans to be interpreted as a concert in support of the politician he had backed in a previous election in 1972—Michael Manley—before his meteoric popular rise in Jamaica. In fact, the government promoted the unity concert, Smile Jamaica, as a collaboration between their cultural affairs office and Marley. Marley didn't oppose or deny that claim.

What became clear to Marley was that any perception of support in one direction or another contradicted his true stance. While Marley promoted Smile Jamaica under the principal objective of unifying the people, the perception persisted that he favored one political party over another. What isn't clear is which party he was perceived to like better. And it also isn't clear who attempted to assassinate him on December 3, 1976.

It could have been representatives of Manley's People's National Party (PNP) as their bodyguards protecting Marley mysteriously disappeared that evening. Or it could have been the Jamaica Labour Party (JLP) as they were unhappy with the idea of the PNP's purported (but never confirmed) support of Marley. Or, it could have been some impatient debt collectors of one of Marley's friends, a Jamaican footballer named Skill Cole, who was in the house at the time.[2]

No one knew who "they" were.

The practice of DEI as it stands has been built and often reinforced via a "We and Dem" paradigm. No one figured out the identity of the "they" who tried to assassinate Marley. And like the song, it is not clear (at least not to me) in doing this work who "they" and "we" are.

I am not completely naïve, nor am I a dogged pessimist. I do my best to be guided by pragmatist's principles.[3] Nonetheless, I'm not neutral when something or someone is deceitful, dishonest, dehumanizing, degrading, or dumb. I consider myself a steward of humanity. The purpose of my life and my work lies in choosing humanity. So, if it is harmful to others, I feel compelled to act.

And yet, the idea of a "them" doesn't make sense to me. At no time in my life has my stance of consciously avoiding the creation of an "other" been challenged as much as it has since the summer of 2020.

COVID-19

We find ourselves in a global pandemic from a novel coronavirus that has infected over two hundred million people worldwide, with over four million deaths. Of those cases, almost 20 percent of them have occurred in my country of birth. The United States has reported over fifty-two million cases and over eight hundred thousand deaths (about 15 percent of global mortality) with a current average, as of this writing, of over one hundred thousand cases and one thousand fatalities per day.

As the author David Berreby said in his book *Us and Them: The Science of Identity*, "Human Beings are amazingly good at finding reasons to believe that we aren't like *them*." Our embedded notions of people and how we classify and type others are not relegated to what we know about them. Our labels and feelings are dictated by what we have and have not been exposed to; the frequency and variations in exposure to particular humankinds. The associations and conclusions we draw fit with what we have "experienced." It matters how and when we were exposed to such data.

In some cases, we have never had direct experience with a particular humankind. All that we know comes from various media sources. For example, if you saw a movie about a being from another galaxy or planet, you may or may not empathize with them. Your ability to accept or reject the *idea* of this being drives your perception of this human or non-humankind.

Think about the title character E.T. from Steven Spielberg's iconic film *E.T. the Extra-Terrestrial*. In the movie, the writers and director spent considerable time in revealing and developing E.T.'s character to make the alien more relatable—from E.T. developing a love for a familiar candy, Reese's Pieces; to learning to talk in English; to experiencing an innocent kiss from six-year-old Gertie (played by Drew Barrymore). Globally, we increasingly related to E.T., despite never having seen a creature like it in real life.

The 2009 movie *District 9* is set in South Africa and begins as a flashback to 1982, when a giant extraterrestrial spaceship arrives and hovers over the South African city of Johannesburg. A million malnourished aliens derogatorily called "Prawns" (an insect indigenous to South Africa and resembling a mix of a grasshopper and roach) are inside. The South African government relocates them to a camp called District 9. Years of neglect and inhumane treatment turns the camp into a slum. Locals complain that the aliens are filthy, ignorant lawbreakers who bleed resources from humans.

Conflict increases between the aliens and locals, and the aliens are relocated. The effort is led by the son-in-law of the CEO of a weapons manufacturer hired for the relocation, Wikus. As relocation is unfolding, an alien named Christopher Johnson (no known relation to the author), his young son CJ, and friend Paul search a District 9 garbage dump for alien fuel found in the extraterrestrial's technology. This was part of a plan to use the fuel to escape Earth and save his kind. Wikus discovers the escape plan and is exposed to the fuel, which causes him to mutate into one of the aliens, starting with his left arm. His employer discovers his change, and they immediately take him to their lab, where they discover his chimeric mutation allows him to use alien weaponry inaccessible to humans.

Wikus fights off his employer and must hide. He flees his family and takes refuge in District 9. Christopher shares that he can help him but they must cooperate. Wikus agrees.

This story takes the viewer from a sense of "them" and "us" to a clear example of the arbitrariness of the notion. Who is "them"? Who is the "other" in this story? It's not easy to answer the question, and the response many would give is, "it depends."

"It depends" is a favorite phrase of my lawyer friends and colleagues. They mostly use it when presented with a question that doesn't have a binary response. That is, most questions of substance.

Christopher and Wikus each saw the other as "them." In Christopher's case, his "them" were those devaluing and subjugating his kind. For Wikus, the "them" were the aliens, a group that was never given a chance to demonstrate their value to society. In the process of what we could say is a transformation of perspective for both of Wikus and Christopher, the otherness faded away as their destinies became interdependent.

This movie leaves me with a sense of hope toward what Berreby calls "kind sight." Kind sight, says Berreby, is something that all humankinds possess. Practicing it means that we can "learn and follow intricate rules for treating people just as, and only as, they should be treated—*given the kind of person they are, and the kind we are, in the situation we meet them.*"

Throughout the year 2020 and into 2021, human beings worldwide have experienced levels of morbidity, mortality, shock, and bewilderment beyond what the planet has ever simultaneously experienced in modern history. The rapid spread of a viral pathogen through nearly every country in the world, to varying degrees, has presented global planetary consciousness with choices.

In the simplified language of public health, these choices were not limited to how we managed to "flatten the curve." They have been and continue to be much more complex. Throughout 2020, as it concerns the USA, the pandemic's devastation was exacerbated by untimely celebrity deaths (particularly that of professional basketball legend Kobe Bryant and his daughter Gianna) and two trials to impeach the president of the United States. And then, in the convergence of the above public mourning, political strife, and panic for the stealth spread of a deadly pathogen, the world witnessed the public lynching of George Floyd by four cops in Minneapolis, Minnesota.

All humans create notions of "them" in our minds. The past year, the list of who "them" is has been both reinforced, like in the political othering that we saw during the impeachment trials of an American president. Or those who found a reason to, while celebrating his life, revisit the past of Kobe Bryant's criminal sexual assault charge in 2003 that was dismissed in 2004. We have reinforced all police as other, and those who support the police and publicly state "Blue Lives Matter" are othered by and othering those who support the "Black Lives Matter" (BLM) movement.

And we have new creations of the other. We have those who believe COVID-19 is a hoax, and some who believe it was "created" by the Chinese. As well as some who, due to disparities in morbidity and mortality, believe it has been invented to harm Black people, similar to myths about HIV that arose in the 1990s and persist in some minds until the present day. Of course, I would be missing a significant othering contest if I didn't discuss the ongoing masked versus unmasked, vaccinated versus unvaccinated farce.

Whether it be notions transferred to us about honoring the dead, respecting or rejecting the role police have in communities, or trusting in the scientific/medical establishment, the othering that we see is associative. It is relevant to all other associations that have encoded our minds via our life experiences and observations of the experiences of others. Had we known these stimuli ahead of time, the responses would have been predictable.

The result of today is not isolated to the now. We have created the present in our response to all that proceeded it. It is no wonder that we are confused as to the indisputable reality that "we" for the first time in my and many others' lifetimes are faced with a definitive "them" that is wreaking havoc on planetary consciousness. It is not sentient, nor is it a humankind. However, it does seek out and live inside of humankinds. In some places in the world, like cancer, we have declared war against it. It has required trillions of dollars to combat its effects. Yet, while our universal "them" COVID-19 continues inflicting trauma on modern civilization, our attention has not brought us to a rare state of transnational solidarity. Instead, it has created for some a new reinforcement of old othering in the form of blame placing and projection. That is the disappointing side of the story, but not the whole story.

The whole story is still being written.

During the US Civil Rights era, there were several events that caused people to pause and consider how they wanted the world to be and how they wanted to be in the world. George Floyd's death and the fact that it was broadcast on social media channels around the world reminds me of how Emmett Till's mother, Mamie Carthan Till, held an open casket funeral for her son and had the *Chicago Defender* and *Jet* magazine print pictures of the corpse, which garnered national attention. Jeff Robinson, racial justice expert for the ACLU, said in 2017 that the murder of Till and the living picture of the fourteen-year-old Emmett alongside a picture of his corpse was a turning point of the Civil Rights movement. He shared that white

Americans began to think, "Yes, those Blacks cause a lot of problems . . . but I didn't sign up for this." One could surmise that George Floyd's virally broadcasted death was a global, modern-day clarion call for civil and human rights that most people in the world had never realized was so critical.

Such a call to action is rare. When I lived in the US, my lack of participating in marches for causes such as Black Lives Matter or other injustices was due to my skeptical, modern-era "realism." I knew without a doubt that real change wouldn't happen in those marches. In fact, I had repeatedly seen the energy die down in a short period of time and life would return to "normal." This time had been different. We marched.

What started in late May of 2020 had continued through the year 2021, with protests large and small happening around the world—movements to make police more accountable to communities; to remove monuments commemorating the antebellum South and other colonialist representations around the world; and to challenge companies to go beyond platitudes of support and move headfirst into humanizing action.

Nonetheless, we have not moved beyond the tendency to make "them" wrong. Many white people at large have been underinformed about the history of their ancestors and, in many cases, their own roles in perpetuating inequity. When your experience has been considered as normative, privilege can be unknowingly and strikingly blinding. There is no excuse, but there is space for advancing the conversation on how to be accountable in a sustainable way. Spending a lot of social capital on "othering" or making people wrong will not move organizations toward equity. In fact, it is likely to trigger the opposite.

Holding power accountable is necessary. There is no evidence that says organizations would have moved in this direction without the concurrence of events starting in 2020. And, if we look at the recent catastrophes as a chance to create systems and structures that can prevent other similar disasters from happening; and/or if our institutions and communities are strengthened rather than diminished by these tragedies, we create something sustainable, beyond typical cosmetic gestures. Many organizations want to be accountable, and they want inclusion to be reflective of who they are. As well, they want to look good. There is no reason why they cannot have both.

Nonetheless, before they can get on the road to making their brand nice and shiny, they must invest in transforming how business is done. This includes how companies hire, procure, develop, compensate/reward, communicate, contribute to the uplift of communities, and much more. In short, they must look at the entirety of their operation and make systemic changes that reflect equity in their purpose, for everyone in the organization including accounting for a history of disparate outcomes for Black people and other subordinated groups.

The above is not meant to be and is not corporate social responsibility. It represents a new way of operating, an approach to organizational life that goes beyond transactional pacification of dissent. It's about building equitable structures for organizational ecosystems. A pivot from "us" and "them" to "We, the architects of this organizational culture, will build our firm with equity in mind. We believe this serves the best interests of all of our stakeholders."

Such statements can be a bit frightening to the classical capitalist. They can occur as far-fetched, unrealistic, and even threatening to what one believes is the purpose of a corporation—profit. As author and professor Alex Edmans says, they can make people feel like DEI equates to "pie-splitting," akin to a zero-sum, lose-win orientation.[4]

In the current times, if an organization wants the organizational purpose solely to revolve around profitability, rising stock, and abundant dividends, I suggest that they don't invest much more in diversity, equity, and inclusion. When a company is only about what they can gain versus what they can deliver beyond extrinsic benefit, investing into their DEI office will result in very little other than being able to check the box, perhaps with additional budget. Many times, the investment can have negative effects because the "why" they invested is rooted in something short-lived. It is not structured for sustainable impact.

The organization won't have a material stake in the prioritization of DEI. Without it, programs to create equity won't be successful. In fact, the efforts will remain as or revert to being the programs for "them"—more than ever before. When organizations don't have a stake in the outcomes, they tolerate passive-aggressive efforts to challenge movements of diverse groups under the guise of free speech. One example of this is the proliferation of "Straight Pride Parades" via the Straight Pride sloganizing that started in the 1980s in reaction to growing acceptance of Gay Pride. Those leading this spread of a meaningless slogan managed to hold parades around the world beginning in 2005 in Canada, to as recently as the summer of 2019 in Boston. Despite the parades being slowed by the pandemic, the group kept their rhetoric alive, pivoting not against the "non-normal gays" (referencing a public photo where they carried signs that said, "Make Normalcy Normal Again," "It's Great to Be Straight," and "Straight Lives Matter") but against those protesting for humanizing the police and safety for Black people. Their cover was that they needed to support their cause. In fact, John Hugo, organizer and president of the group Super Happy Fun America, said, "Enough already, it's time to support the police."[5]

Identity politics is an intermediary of "othering." While being for a particular humankind doesn't require finding an opposite to be against, it can easily move in that direction if group identity is threatened.

Ken Gergen, perhaps the most critical scholar in social constructionist thought, says: "At the outset, the [predominant] rhetoric has been of little influence outside groups of the already committed. [For those who seem in need of] political education—such rhetoric has more often been alienating or counter-productive. By and large identity politics has depended on a rhetoric of blame, the [intended] effects of which are designed to chastise the target (for being unjust, prejudiced, inhumane, selfish, oppressive, and/or violent). In western culture we essentially [possess] two conversational responses to such forms of chastisement—[join them or oppose them.]"[6]

How do organizations truly establish an unambiguous prioritization of an inclusive culture? Dedicating resources to a parade is a nice, symbolic gesture. I suggest organizations participate in such events as they send signals of an organization's aspirations and intentions—a movement toward solidarity. It is an incomplete gesture if it is not combined with other deliberate efforts. In contributing to events or causes seen as valuable, organizations have an avenue to articulate their beliefs in a diverse citizenry. Not in a way that says, "you must do this." Rather in the way of an invitation. In a manner that says:

> This is who we are. We believe all should feel as if we belong. We do things consistently to make this consistently be the case. Your beliefs are your beliefs. If any of the actions of your beliefs are unhelpful or not safe for everyone in the organization, they are not acceptable. We trust that you will observe when we behave in ways reflecting our values and purpose, and we trust that when you observe an incidence of this not being the case, that you will bring it to the attention of the parties involved. And, if you cannot find your way back to "This is who we are" together, please bring it to the attention of a senior colleague or directly to me.
>
> —Sincerely, Your CEO

The fictional CEO statement above intentionally includes everyone. Consider not including "them" (unless those are preferred pronouns for an individual) in your organization. Simply include everyone. It seems counterintuitive. "Diverse" people (e.g., someone representing an ERG) might say, "If 'they' are there, people may not feel safe." To which I would respond, "Do you want people to feel safe with everyone?" The answer: "Yes, of course." And I would conclude with, "Great. Then it makes sense to include everyone." Yet, such a statement alone is insufficient without action.

Keeping people separated into identity groups to feel safe is similar to social distancing to prevent the spread of a pathogen. It doesn't create the "socialness" that holds the potential to shift the contexts that contribute to systemic inequities. What it does do, unintentionally, is reinforce the invisible barriers that hinder connection and relatedness across humankinds. There is no agreed-upon evidence that this works across a variety of environments. This doesn't make it wrong, but it requires that we explore its actions to assure that the construct serves our organizations and communities.

Organizational statements or even the formation of programs don't necessarily move people toward a more significant ability to learn and grow their collective impact. They may affirm a defined group's confidence in their individual or collective standing in an organization for some time. However, such assurance is likely temporary if it is constructed for one group without intentional actions that invite perspectives for the purpose of sustaining the group's aspirations. Ambitions that are often related to the reparations (or at least reconciliation) of some sort for systemic disparities. You cannot maintain a systemic change without the collective action of many stakeholders working in solidarity.

Thinking that it is possible to go it alone from the perspective of a particular humankind is erroneous and ironic. Consider this statement: "We don't hate anyone; *we* just want to have *our own* celebration just like *everybody else* has a right to. All people from all communities are welcome as long as they show mutual respect." This is a reasonable statement. Right? Many groups have felt the urge to exercise their respective stances in a public display. This statement comes from the organizer of the Straight Pride Parade (mentioned above) that was approved by the city of Boston in 2019 and went forward August 31 of that year.

Whether one agrees that such an event is reactive and antagonistic to Gay Pride is irrelevant here, and what is relevant is that they do have the right to such a display. And while I think that a statement-making parade about that which is societally normative is silly, their rights to express their affirmation on a public stage are no less valid than the liberating displays from the LGBTQA+ community.

So where does this leave us? Where inclusion, diversity, and equity are concerned, we remain in a binary "othered" state contrary to what we can all claim to be humanistic pursuits. However, the practice of "othering" is not humanistic. Obviously, this is not a confirmation that inhumane treatment is acceptable. I am sickened when I think of Emmett Till, George Floyd, Breonna Taylor, Serena Angelique Velázquez, and Layla Pelaez Sánchez,[7] all brutally murdered with their identities playing at least an implicit role in the perpetrators' decision-making.

Nonetheless, the world is much more complex than the essentialist-like assignment of such behaviors to a particular group. To state that a monolithic notion of "they" (in many cases white men) is perpetuating inhumanity and then commence to an ideological takedown, based on particular facets of identity with expectations and intentions to inspire change, is absurd. This combativeness is not what organizations, nor the myriad humankinds that operate within them, seek to create.

David Berreby speaks of science in a way that also captures a theme of organizational life: "If the theme of science for the last five hundred years could be boiled down into a sentence, it would be this: the world is not what you believe it is." I would add that, "The other is not the other you believe them to be, either."

Let's return to the fundamentals of an Inclusion System. The notion of a "them" is illusionary. I do not mean that there aren't behaviors or personalities that are so contaminating that they don't have to be singled out and given a proper detox. The cases where this happens should be comparatively few. I would compare them to hospitalized breakthrough (fully vaccinated people contracting) COVID-19 cases, which are a very small percentage of all hospitalized cases.

If the objective is to create an organization whose people thrive through inclusive actions, there needs to be a movement away from any form of "us vs. them" binaries. They are contrary to all the foundational elements of an Inclusion System, starting with the first one that talks about inclusion being *accessible to everyone* in an organization. It is critical that we are intentional and unambiguously prioritize creating solidarity across humankinds, investing in organizational efforts toward care/community, openness, safety, and trust, or your organizational efforts will never be sustainable.

In fact, any subtle, conscious, or unconscious actions toward creating a lane for blame and/or othering will exhaust DEI efforts. Such fatigue is created when we develop frameworks for DEI that are incomplete. Building approaches that don't hold promise for the betterment of everyone in our organizations create missed opportunities. If the DEI journey isn't constantly adjusting in order to evolve beyond our relatively modest expectations (e.g., increased representation, ignorance not being surfaced), what purpose do our efforts serve?

Let me be clear that the intentions and aspirations that we have had as so-called DEI practitioners are affirmatively extraordinary. Equal if not greater emphasis should be put on the outputs, the aspirational impacts, the effect—not the causes alone. What that means is that we must be mindful about our inputs. That is, our behavioral, structural, and systemic learning and actions that move us toward what we desire versus a predominant emphasis on dismantling what we don't want.

In the development of an inclusion system, we root for everyone. As we do so, it becomes much easier to root the notion of "them" out of the organizational mind. Moving from the old paradigm of binarity to one of wholeness is part of the critical path of creating cultures that thrive via inclusion.

Meritocracy

> "The human brain has no mechanism to recognize what is relevant or what is not. Relevance is an environmental/cultural phenomenon. All value is actualized through imagination alone."
>
> **—Joseph Campbell**

Whether one agrees with Joseph Campbell or not, knowing what is significant—and, more importantly, why it is so—is an age-old phenomenon that I believe few of us have taken the time to closely examine. Scholars have studied the nature of belief systems. Similar to Campbell's quote, they have concluded that the context and content of an individual, made up of their biases and in some cases sacred beliefs, determines their "belief" in something.

The ideas we have about things, circumstances, and people can change ("hindsight is 20/20" or more recently the year 2020), but if we look at our overall beliefs as objectively as we can, most of them are made up. We concluded them to be significant or relevant via relative context and, perhaps more frequently, our current satisfaction or dissatisfaction with our (and our communities') circumstances. If you review public statements of politicians, you will see the extremes of how this idea is applied.

Meritocracy is an idea that has stood the test of time, even though it was a term first published to serve as satire and a quasi-warning about our anchoring on such an ideal. As defined, "the holding of power (or influence) by people selected on the basis of their ability," meritocracy makes sense. In theory, I agree that a person who has intentionally sharpened insights and skills in a particular discipline, vocation, or toward solving an intractable challenge should be granted opportunities to engage in their work at higher levels and should be proportionally rewarded to do so.

This does not mean that everyone except the most qualified candidate is doomed, or that one's merit is equal to one's worth. What it means is that the most qualified candidate should be offered the best position and be compensated accordingly, and that less qualified candidates should be placed in positions that better suit their qualifications and capabilities. It also means that someone's network (i.e., your family, closest friends, and people they know) does not guarantee a ticket to a high-level opportunity for self-gain. That is "capability + effort = merit," not "exposure + network + capability + effort = superior merit."

Understanding meritocracy as a myth is important as you develop an Inclusion System in your organization. I frame it as a requirement in developing an Inclusion System because of how much performance and talent management systems conceptually rely on it. When something is so ever-present, it is easy to believe that it's a complete idea and can be continued without scrutiny. This is not the case and thus requires deeper exploration.

The ideal of meritocracy could be like D. H. Lawrence's beliefs about the notion of ideals: "Our crimes and perversities are only possible because we have put ourselves in the service of ideals, and lost our souls in the process." I am not sure if I would line up meritocracy with "crimes and perversities," but I would agree in part that the obsession with the ideal of merit has created a belief among some that it is only the best of the best that are rewarded with the most. Meritocracy, while receiving a theoretical thumbs-up from most, is far from ideal. In fact, if we look at merit-based systems such as the performance management and promotion systems of many corporations, we can easily see that the ideal of meritocracy is flawed. Even if we agree that the concept of meritocracy is viable and useful in organizational systems, doing so without exploring the dark side of the concept is shortsighted and too often leads to fostering inequity. Michael Young, who is accredited with coining the term, explores the dark side of the idea in his 1958 satire, *The Rise of the Meritocracy*.[1]

The Myth

Michael Young was a sociologist, social reformist, and educator. He is credited with drafting large parts of the manifesto "Let Us Face the Future" in 1945, which led to an increase in adult education, free secondary school education, the National Health Service, and universal social security. The reforms also lead to the establishment of unions and labor laws. These laws reduced the hours that laborers worked and increased wages, giving working-class families a better quality of life and greater incomes. The result of all this was a marked rise in the lifestyle of the English middle and upper classes. Their opportunities for leisure expanded, as did the possibilities to invest in their children's future, which resulted in their ability to move up the occupational hierarchy.

Ironically, the reform that Young's work inspired was also a partial cause of the social inequities that he spent his life fighting. As more people became upwardly mobile, more children were left with greater inheritances. And with that, the possibilities for structural inequities via access to generational wealth grew exponentially, especially as educational opportunities and networks formed as an outgrowth of these conditions.

Young anticipated these unintended consequences, and *The Rise of the Meritocracy* was written as a warning of the possible negative outcomes of the reforms. The narrator in the story reflects that "nearly all parents are going to try to gain *unfair* advantages for their offspring." Coupled with those advantages would be associating oneself with those who are of similar status via marriage, having access to opportunities for financial gain (i.e., jobs, capital, networks), and pursuing educational opportunities at elite educational institutions.

Young's satire was not interpreted as the mockery of the English elites who believed that their privilege was justified. Instead, they anchored on to it as a neutral ideal. Rather than taking Young's critique and shortcomings into consideration, meritocracy came to mean that outcomes were fair—even when the playing field was qualitatively imbalanced and reinforced to advantage one's closest connections from the beginning. Instead of weakening the notion, it was reinforced by those who historically were of greater privilege, to believe that their ongoing reaping of rewards over many generations was simply because they "deserved" it. Those who accumulated more wealth, status, or access to power (significantly more) than others were further convinced (many still are) by the idea that their merit was superior to others who had accumulated fewer extrinsic rewards. This belief has been relentlessly reinforced in societies and companies for so long that, despite what we have learned about bias and repeatedly articulated intentions toward organizational equity, it persists.

Myths are important to human development. They help us make sense of what we don't understand and deepen our experience of the awe of the multiverse. Myths as stories may or may not be true, yet their purpose goes beyond a black-and-white notion of true and false. Like stereotypes, which many interpret as negative or untrue, myths are incomplete without deep reflection and a willingness to be influenced beyond one's fixed beliefs. This doesn't mean that one should reflect and then believe. In fact, with meritocracy, it might be more valuable to approach it in a way that allows us to see its mythological qualities and what they can teach us, versus debating whether to accept it as mythology in the first place.

Even thirty years after his death, Joseph Campbell remains the foremost expert on myths. Campbell articulated that myths have four functions: mystical, cosmological, sociological, and pedagogical. He maintained that the sociological function, which supports and validates social order while being the most prevalent in society today, is problematic. The sociological function's role has been in validating a fixed social order based on rules that are often no longer contextually relevant.

An example of the outdatedness of Campbell's sociological function are the myths of Pandora (Ancient Greece) and Eve (Judeo-Christianity). The stories have great similarity. Both place women at the center of the problems that exist for humankind and assign men the role of fixing those problems. When myths such as Pandora and Eve can lead to oppression, they are the opposite of what we would claim to want in contemporary society. Meritocracy, despite its good intentions at inception, has been held up as a societal standard. At best, though, it's incomplete. At its worst, it's dehumanizing. With such a range, it helps us to look at it from Campbell's fourth function of myths, the pedagogical angle. Here myths, as tools, teach and guide us through life. This function helps us make sense of myths in relation to our lived experience. That is, when we encounter situations that require deeper understanding, the pedagogical function reveals meaning and can spark an "aha" moment toward new insights and a path(s) forward.[2]

Conceptually, a clear understanding of meritocracy holds the potential to help individuals and organizations see equity, the "E" in DEI, in a different light. Through deconstructing meritocracy, mainly separating the ideal from the reality of how it's been practiced, we can reconsider how this notion has served the people in our organizations. You can then ask: Has the idea of meritocracy helped people thrive? If yes, who has it helped (more or less)? Where does it serve or hinder our mission? Does our current perception of it help us create a generative culture? If yes, what is the evidence of this outcome?

Many believe that meritocracy is ethical, rational, and just. On paper, they could be right. Judging people on their intellect, consistent effort, and impact makes sense. That they get what they proportionally deserve seems reasonable. The problem with this interpretation of meritocracy is that it is interpreting a metaphorical ideal as a fact. This is problematic because metaphors, as we all know, are not facts. As Campbell says, it would be like going to a restaurant asking for a particular food from the menu and then proceeding to eat the menu. It is not guaranteed to satisfy your hunger. Similarly, meritocracy, although integrated into business practices as factual, is not a proxy for fairness. This is the reality, even though many have been led to believe it serves that very purpose.

In a 2010 study, MIT professor Emilio Castilla found that emphasizing meritocratic values at an organizational level had a counterintuitive effect. In his study, he had participants take on the role of managers. One group was provided a set of core values that emphasized meritocracy. The other group was not. The results were perhaps not so surprising given what we have learned about bias, but they were paradoxical. The study found that those participants primed for meritocratic values when assessing compensation rewarded male employees a bonus that was, on average, about 12 percent higher than females. Conversely, those participants who were not primed for meritocracy rewarded women a bonus of about 13 percent more than men.[3]

The authors called this counterintuitive result the "paradox of meritocracy"—a situation "where people can show greater levels of gender bias when they are in a context that emphasized meritocracy." They continue to state that the irony in this is that when an organization or entity emphasizes meritocracy, it could lull individuals into a false belief that their decisions are unbiased because, theoretically, meritocracies are inherently fair.

Yet, the priming led the participants to make biased decisions simply because they felt justified based on the context constructed by the researchers. In the case of an organization, it would be those who articulate and communicate meritocracy as a core organizational belief who play the role of context creators.

If we go back to the metaphor of the myth, we can find similarities between religious myth (and local legends) and meritocracy. It serves the value of informing us about what can be. We appreciate such a possibility, and sometimes we come to see it as Truth. But the purpose of myths is not to be the (capital "T") Truth. In fact, myths are often not true. Rather, the purpose of a myth is to take something into deep consideration to see how close one can move toward the higher aspirations of a story vs. the dark side that leaves people stuck with fixed notions that are often the antithesis of its core value.

The story of a colleague of mine speaks to the inconsistent nature of the meritocracy myth. We will call her Hope for this example. Hope entered Spelman College, which is a women's historically Black college (HBCU) based in Atlanta. The high school she went to was not science, technology, engineering, and math (STEM) oriented. So, when she came to college, she was behind many of her classmates academically. However, the difference between many of her classmates and her was that she absolutely loved science. She knew she wanted to work as a scientist. She was not hoping to go to medical school or to take her science degree and do something else; she wanted to be a scientist.

While many of her classmates were getting recognized for their grades and receiving scholarships and internships related to research careers, most knew they wanted to be physicians, not researchers. Hope maintained her focus. She graduated from college and then went and got her PhD in biology at another HBCU. Following this, she did a post-doc in a great lab, where the principal investigator who hired her saw her potential when many others only focused on her pedigree.

What she found there, like in college, was that many of the post-docs in her lab who advanced fastest through publications and being invited to be a part of the most popular projects had parents, grandparents, and a broad network of scientists who they'd been mentored and coached by for years. They routinely had dinner with top (sometimes Noble Prize–nominated) scientists and had done so their entire lives. Many had done several traineeships with some of the most well-known researchers in their discipline because of who they knew. Yes, they were smart. But they weren't *smarter*. They were *more exposed*.

Hope's aptitude was not in question. She worked as hard, and I would say harder because she often felt that she had to make up for the gaps that started prior to her entering college. She saw a few gaps while at Spelman, and, through her own self-study, great professors, and perseverance, elevated herself and could confidently enter a PhD program. After graduate school, she recognized other underexposure gaps and went about solving how she could close them, identifying the skills that could position her for the career she envisioned.

Hope wouldn't have been the "best of the best" candidate in many organizations. Without graduate school and post-doc labs with mentors who invested in her potential, she would have likely been overlooked. The fixed notions of how to evaluate talent-by-pedigree and -network that too many organizations consider merit-based would have evaluated her based on what is often exclusive criteria—full of requirements mirrored by those who created and are disproportionally advantaged by them.

Today, Hope is a member of the senior executive service, among the top executives in the United States Department of Health and Human Services. Her effort has been rewarded. She started with considerably less exposure to her career path than others and eventually proved herself. Hope worked hard, but she also built relationships with people who came to believe not predominantly in her pedigree, but in her potential. Hope always had merit, but it took more time to encounter people who created the space for her merit to shine.

Hope is one of the good stories. For every Hope, there are thousands of people with great potential who don't have the fortune or mentors who recognize them. Too many who cannot get a foot in the door, not because they lack qualifications, but the social capital and exposure to networks that can shine light on a path forward.

Meritocracy is an admirable myth. It's not a standard we can stand by as an absolute. So, when we think about meritocracy in the context of DEI, it is indeed a paradox as Castilla and others describe above. In their experiment, they got the opposite of what they expected upon observation.

Thinking that you are being fair doesn't mean that you *are* being fair. At least not for everyone.

Resistance

In 2001, about a year prior to his death, Michael Young wrote an essay reinforcing the fact that his 1958 original text was satire and that what he feared would happen had come to fruition. He wrote the essay in protest to the contemporary British system, at the time under the leadership of Prime Minister Tony Blair, whose cabinet Young described as being full of meritocrats—elites who uniformly believed that their advancement was the result of their own merits and not disproportionally influenced by elite educational advantages and reinforced proportionally to the "amazing battery of certificates and degrees at its disposal," as Young stated.[4]

He saw the perpetuation of the ideal of meritocracy gripping the minds of the country's citizens in a way that caused inherent inequality, as articulated in his satirical narrative.

"I expected that the poor and the disadvantaged would be done down, and in fact they have been . . . ," Young said. "In the new social environment, the rich and the powerful have been doing mighty well for themselves. They have been freed from the old kinds of criticism from people who had to be listened to. This once helped keep them in check . . . The business meritocracy is in vogue. If meritocrats believe, as more and more of them are encouraged to, that their advancement comes from their own merits, they can feel they deserve whatever they can get . . . [They] believe they have morality on their side."

So, Young's resistance related to his term "meritocracy" and his sense of its insidiousness is dismissed by those who benefit the most from perpetuating his original satire as a contemporary, moral truth.

During the past fifty years, many organizations have been simultaneously working toward establishing meritocracy and committing to increased representation of underrepresented groups. The conflict here is obvious. If you have worked in an organization for any period, you have heard someone say, "We *just* want the best candidate." In this regard, people are dealing with a false dichotomy: best versus different. If the best candidate happens to be different than the predominant archetype, the default is often that difference seems like it is not in alignment with the narrative of a meritorious value system.

Few people (including Young and myself) would resist a truly merit-based system. The problem is that there is no such thing. If there were, I imagine all of us would be inquiring about how to construct it. And if it had been created prior to Young's death, without a doubt he would have written a follow-up to his satire, proclaiming that it was indeed possible to create an untainted meritocratic structure for an organization or institution.

In a story about Young, writer and scholar Kwame Anthony Appiah states: "We go wrong when we deny not only the merit but the dignity of those whose luck in the genetic lottery and in the historical contingencies of their situation has left them less rewarded." He continued articulating that wealth and status rewards will always be unequal. However, the idea that all children should have access to a decent education and exposure to opportunities suitable to their talents and choices; and ultimately that all this should be done with the idea that all children should be able to regard themselves with self-respect [is possible and achievable].[5]

While we are far from this dynamic in most parts of the world, resistance to the ideal of meritocracy must persist and remain a sociological myth that instructs us on what not to do rather than what we can hold onto as reflective of an egalitarian principle. Conversely, there will be those who believe in the mythological idea and oppose those who champion equity while perpetuating the adverse impact of an erroneous ideal.

Making DEI accessible, actionable, and sustainable requires rethinking meritocracy. It means resisting the idea that it benefits everyone. One may explain:

I resist the notion of meritocracy being complete. My resistance lies in the historical and present-day potential for harm to be done when organizations are overconfident "meritocracies." I resist inherently inequitable notions of meritocracy because everyone has merit, and everyone deserves dignity. I resist because of the potential for harm when influential actors in organizations insist on their preferences for a particular job candidate profile (often similar to theirs) or pedigree. And these individuals do so while organizations publicly pronounce that equity is a desired outcome. I resist because we are likely doing the same and that is unacceptable. Holding on to this notion doesn't serve us. Rather than anchor on meritocracy, we will anchor on developing our people. We will anchor on the boundless potential of one another.

Sincerely, Your CEO

Organizations committed to equity should resist the hardwired idea of meritocracy, just as this fictional CEO does. This resistance shouldn't necessarily be based on morals or notions of rightness or wrongness. Rather, resistance to the myth of meritocracy can be a component in your ongoing surveillance for fairness. When you see meritocratic ideals masking themselves in people's preferences, organizational traditions, or what is expedient—question the motivation and/or the intended outcome. Question whether decisions made from systems designed for meritocracy are clear, consistent, and caring. If they are not, inequity is likely in process or being reinforced in the organizational mind.

Closing the Gap: From Meritocracy to Inclusion

Justus von Liebig was a German chemical botanist who died in 1873. His contributions are many, including being considered the "Father of Fertilizer" for his discoveries in the area of agriculture. He discovered marmite by determining that brewer's yeast could be concentrated, put in a container, and consumed. He also co-discovered chloroform, which has many uses, including as a surgical anesthetic.

Dr. Liebig's research was vast, and one particular theory that he hypothesized is called Liebig's Law of the Minimum (Liebig's Law). Originally referring to plant systems, Liebig's Law states that growth is dictated not by the total resources available, but by the resource that is in least supply. Stated in another, more familiar way, "a chain is only as strong as its weakest link."[6] In an organizational context, the sustained growth of an organization depends on every link.

Liebig's theory has likely not been regularly associated with organizations. However, when we look at it in an organizational context, we could say the same thing. There is always a weakest link. Assuming each link or component represents an individual, growth of the firm is equivalent to how everyone has developed, like how each link would be strengthened.

The growth of an organization is dependent on the strengthening of its *least plentiful* component. And, if the organization wants to continue to grow, it must consistently deconstruct and strengthen all its components. Only then will organizational capacity for change, agility, leadership, velocity, innovation, and collaboration expand. When we think about organizations and their people via a purported system of meritocracy, Liebig's Law is contrarian. In fact, when people get a low rating in organizations, they often become targets for dismissal. Instead of being strengthened, the weakest link is eliminated. It is a flawed process that leaves people less than empowered and eventually causes harm to the entire organization.

When a low performer is ranked at the end of a year, they begin the next year worried about their future in the company. The result is like a self-fulfilling prophecy, as their fear drives them rather than their goals and purpose inspiring them. The employee begins a vicious cycle, thinking, "Due to my low performance rating, I am now considered not so good." With that premise, HR works with the manager to start a performance improvement process (PIP), which lays out everything that employee must do in alignment with the manager's desires. The so-called PIP usually isn't really about performance improvement. It is about justification of the manager's decision to move this person out of their line of sight as quickly and efficiently as possible while appearing to be impartial. PIPs are a farce.

I once was asked to do a PIP for someone on my team. My manager indicated that a more senior executive had the impression—based on a half-hour meeting—that someone on my team seemed as if "they didn't have it all together and that they weren't [sufficiently] passionate about their role." The result was a suggestion that my team member be placed into some protocol to prove that they still had what it took to remain a member of my team.

At first, it was hard for me to believe the senior executive could make that assessment in thirty minutes. It seemed premature, and I was grateful that my boss didn't immediately consent and proceed down the road of dismissal, as so often happens when an executive makes such comments about an individual. Then, in response to the PIP, I said that I would not do it like a traditional HR-driven process. I refused to call it a PIP or frame it as punitive for my team member.

Instead, I spoke openly with the team member about the situation, where they were, where they would like to improve, and how I could help. I also talked about areas where I saw growth potential. We regularly had conversations from the beginning of their reporting to me. Now, we were making it more deliberate and formal for stakeholders to have an account and be accountable ourselves.

We formally checked in around growth areas every two weeks. Informally, we talked about whom they could learn from and how they could refine specific skills. Our formal conversations were short, summarizing their work, exploring their engagement on projects, and their next steps. The informal discussions were about the how and where. How did they feel about the interactions? How might they think if they did it a bit differently or engaged with a few different people and perhaps more critical stakeholders who could give a record of their experiences? Where were they getting the most value from their action learning, and where else could they tap into similar energy?

The result was what some viewed as a complete turnaround. But was it? It was not a turnaround—it was a more deliberate path for development and growth. It wasn't a plan to improve low performance. If we want to be explicit, we should all have development plans independent of what a performance management system prescribes. There is always space to grow and areas to improve one's performance and impact.

Ask a professional athlete in any sport. They will tell you that their daily goal, game after game, practice after practice, is to improve performance. Whether they have a bad game or a good game, their objective is to keep getting better.

In organizational life, this is not consistently the framing. It should be (and I use the word "should" sparingly). And, if you are making your organization one where inclusion is normative (i.e., a system of inclusion), it is a must.

I believe that companies will benefit from acting according to Liebig's Law rather than contrary to it. This means that they will spend their energy strengthening the capacity of the "substance" in least abundance rather than getting rid of it or creating a process that diminishes it even further. In organizational terms, it means releasing the mindset of erasing low performers— low performers are a natural and unavoidable consequence of measuring performance to begin with. Therefore, the organizational turn should be toward developing all employees and giving them tools to grow and succeed.

Michael Hyter, a pioneer in the DEI space, would agree with developing everyone in an organization. In fact, he states that "we need to replace our current system of meritocracy with another approach—a system of inclusion based on the assumption that almost every employee is talented enough to contribute to our business objectives and that our role as managers is to nurture and develop the talents of all our employees, not only the 'talented few.'"[7] Hyter, without saying he is a proponent of Liebig's Law, indicates that he would also see Liebig's Law as it relates to inclusion.

As far as solutions are concerned, each organization may have different approaches. However, the principles that Hyter lays out as integral for a system of inclusion are universally applicable. He describes three things:

1. *Believe that most people are capable of high levels of performance.*
   In this regard, Hyter encourages organizations to believe in the
   potential of everyone to grow and contribute at a high-level. This is
   a mindset. There's a reason people were hired in the first place, and it
   was to do a job and do it well. They are not necessarily always that top
   10 to 15 percent in the performance management scores. Obviously,
   most are not. However, the belief that everyone is capable of performing at high levels neutralizes the organizational faux pas of giving the
   lion's share of work to the "cream of the crop." The end result is that,
   yes, the top-rated tier performs, but they also can get burned out and
   at some point go from the cream on the top to the sediment at the
   bottom. This happens as a result of their virtues being weighed down
   by organizational pressure and lacking adequate complementary skills
   from their colleagues who don't have the highest performance ratings.

2. *Position everyone for growth and development.*
   Hyter highlights the idea of "position," which he frames as the nature
   of assignments given and the quality of support received, as well as
   individuals growing their understanding of how their responsibilities are connected to fulfilling the organizational mission and business objectives. Hyter states that, "Not only does such Positioning
   benefit the bottom line, it also impacts that person's 'Disposition.'"
   This positive impact on the idea of "disposition" is closely related to
   what many of my colleagues might see as a feeling of "belonging."
   When people feel like they can learn, their confidence grows, their
   commitment deepens, and they become determined to stretch for
   more of that feeling.

3. *Coach performance based on clearly defined standards.*
   Winning teams are often teams that are supportive and act as
   coaches with one another. This is not restricted to those having the
   title of "coach." If one looks at historically great teams, they had
   coaches and players that were clear about what the team needed to
   win and what the various roles could learn, share, and do to best

contribute to their success. Peer coaching is perhaps one of the better capability-building inputs in an Inclusion System.[8] Everyone learns, social capital is elevated, and the probability of creating extraordinary results is raised because of intentionally working toward everyone's growth rather than the development of an exclusive minority.

Coaches, as Hyter shares, "[take] the time to think through and communicate clear expectations . . . ensuring that employees focus their effort on what's important to the business." Hyter continues stating that while many managers feel like they are good at the above, their propensity is to remain rooted in fixed notions of what great performers and performance looks like. The result is that they default to coaching everyone in alignment with a mental model of the organizational status quo, which many will equate with what is meritorious. The result is vague and ambiguous direction, spotty sharing of critical information, and ongoing assessment based on loose, biased, and unhelpful criteria.

If your managers lead with a coaching style based on team members' strengths, a laser focus on business strategy, and how each member can improve, then you are well on your way to a system of inclusion. Systems based on meritocracy won't help you fulfill the promise of each organizational actor developing and making a meaningful contribution. Those with a system of inclusion as their foundation can and more likely will.

▮▮▮

In developing an Inclusion System, coming to an understanding about what meritocracy is—a myth—is important. Without making this clear, a system of meritocracy, which by its nature is a system of exclusion, will compromise your intention to build an Inclusion System.

There are approaches to shifting away from the meritocratic ideal. First, believe in the potential of your employees. That is, if you see an instance where your reports or peers drop in performance, don't conclude that they have reached some imaginary ceiling that cannot be broken through. Consider in all cases that if they aren't able to make a breakthrough in performance alone, then they can with the right help from their management and peers.

Secondly, clearly define standards for employees, and coach them to move toward these standards. Coaching should come from superiors, managers, and peers. Great teams get better together. Developing organizational capacity for people to be helpful coaches with one another is an investment that will provide substantial returns.

Thirdly, develop everyone at every level. Remember Liebig's Law of the Minimum and make sure that development and growth are not dependent on discrete performance ratings. If this is not clear, refer to the first point: believe in the potential of your people. And remember foundational element number one in developing an Inclusion System—its purpose is to help all stakeholders thrive and contribute their best to a generative culture and the organizational mission.

Intersectionality:
The Good, Bad, Ugly, Good

"Look at my arm! I have ploughed and planted and gathered into barns, and no man could head me—and ain't I a woman? I could work as much and eat as much as a man—when I could get it—and bear the lash as well! And ain't I a woman? I have born thirteen children, and seen most of 'em sold into slavery, and when I cried out with my mother's grief, none but Jesus heard me—and ain't I a woman?"

—**Sojourner Truth**

The Good

Invoking the women's rights activist, abolitionist truth-teller, and feminist Isabella Baumfree, who we know historically as Sojourner Truth, is important for two reasons as we discuss intersectionality. The first reason is that Truth's 1851 "Ain't I a woman?" speech, where the above passage comes from, underscores the binaries that predominate our lives on a scale never experienced before. For Truth, it was the question of "Who (in fact) is considered a woman?" For Truth, this was not merely about one's femaleness. Rather, it was about a more complete and significant description of *who* she was as a woman.

Contentious binarity, the notion that someone or something could only identify with one attribute or another, was in operation then. It operated subtly, in a similar manner to the current day, ironically enough. In fact, social media algorithms only seem to perpetuate and reinforce binary thinking. This is not to point a finger at social media as the only accountable party. It simply serves as a mirror to our reductionist framing of the world.

The second reason for starting with Truth is the importance of the question she poses. Truth's question speaks to how people are categorized in the world and how they would choose to be seen. In articulating her multiple identities in the world, Truth could be considered both inwardly contemplative and outwardly condemning. She contradicts what was considered the default at that time about *all women* being fragile and weak, and at the same time speaks to those feminine traits—mother, mourner, of God's faithful— she possesses in parallel with the trope of white women.

In Professor Kimberlé Crenshaw's "Demarginalizing the Intersection of Race and Sex: A Black Feminist Critique of Antidiscrimination Doctrine, Feminist Theory and Antiracist Politics,"[1] where she coins the term "intersectionality," she introduces Sojourner Truth as she starts to critique patriarchy, white feminists, Black men, and the anti-racism movement. Her criticism is not meant to portray these groups as being out of touch. Rather, she pinpoints several examples where they fail to acknowledge and account for the double binds that Black women face in a manner that is both quantitatively and qualitatively credible.

There are many critics of intersectionality. I will discuss their positions later, thus the bad and the ugly of the various interpretations of intersectionality. Yet, even among critics, when asked about the foundational premise of Professor Crenshaw's work, there is little to no disagreement about it making sense. One rabidly conservative commentator and critic, Ben Shapiro, shared with *Vox*'s Jane Coaston that he can agree that Crenshaw's original idea is accurate and unproblematic. Rather, those in opposition are deeply concerned by the practice of intersectionality and what they interpret intersectionality would ask, or demand, of them and of society.[2]

In the same article by Coaston, Crenshaw describes intersectionality as operating as both the observance and analysis of power imbalances and as the tool by which those power imbalances could be eliminated altogether. In conclusion, Coaston states, "And the observance of power imbalances, as is so frequently true, is far less controversial than the tool that could eliminate them."

What Coaston and others have gathered from Crenshaw's interviews and speeches is that the central premise of the work is not to create a reconstructed hierarchy where Black women hold the lion's share of power—an often unspoken perception and reason for resistance. Rather, the intention of her work has been to deconstruct racial hierarchy altogether.

I first encountered the seminal work of Professor Crenshaw's theory of intersectionality in 1999. Published in the *University of Chicago Legal Forum* in 1989, it was my first exposure to the theoretical underpinnings of her work. In the few years prior to reading it for the first time, in college and especially during graduate school via exposure to critical race theory (CRT, also coined by Crenshaw with others) and anti-oppression education, I was primed for what intersectionality represented. Its central premise invigorated my orientation toward thinking about the complexities that lie in social determinants of health—in other words, the idea that health disparities were the result of multiple factors.

The work has also been an element of centering my approach to making inclusion accessible, actionable, and sustainable. As I was once quoted saying by David Livermore, "Diversity is . . . It is what we do with it is what I am most interested in."[3]

Upon inspection, every person is multidimensional. Hidden within the complexities of our identities is the truth that we must reconcile—societal structures and historical constructs have created disparities of agency based on what, mathematically and biologically speaking, are random combinations of differences. This doesn't mean that it is the "fault" of a particular intersectional humankind, like those who are white, male, and heterosexual. However, most who oppose intersectionality do so in resistance to the misinterpretation often found on college campuses and in so-called liberal rhetoric. Critics do not oppose the claim that people are treated, at minimum, differently than others based on appearance and social position. They reject the insinuation that it is the fault of people who have characteristics phenotypically like their own.

Rather, the focus of many of those who push back against intersectionality is on antagonizing an idea that seemingly threatens social and economic hierarchy—a hierarchy that socioeconomically awards disproportional benefit to middle- and upper-class white men in the US and beyond. The criticism itself is not at issue; all theories should be tested and retested to examine their viability in front of an ever-shifting context. This is at the heart of healthy scholarship and civic debate. As one of Professor Crenshaw's former graduate students said, "[Crenshaw is] not really concerned with shallow questions of identity and representation but . . . more interested in the deep structural and systemic questions about discrimination and inequality." Most critics are not interested in such depth. To underscore their lack of interest in deeper societal questions, some have signaled their beliefs by prefacing or concluding their criticism with mention of their predominant identity (mostly white and male).

This is not new, nor has it ceased. In the current mood of the US and, to an extent, around the world, the protests in response to the lynching of George Floyd by a cop's knee pressed against his neck for eight minutes and forty-six seconds in Minneapolis have mostly consisted of peaceful protests. And while the overwhelming global response to the protests and the Black Lives Matter movement has been positive, the reductionist rhetoric (that the problems of society are all about racism) and misconstrued narrative (that addressing the dehumanization of Black people only benefits Black people) has once again fueled an intentional distraction from a global problem that will persist until it is addressed by all that are impacted by it. That means everyone around the world, you and your various humankinds included.

The Bad

Perpetual antagonism toward progressive movements is not new. There have been various groups of people since the end of slavery who have taken on the role of the opposition in causes and ideas that promote equity. Their unstated intention, coupled with sleight-of-hand tactics, has been to spend considerable effort to delegitimize movements, theories, and even legislative mechanisms aimed at creating greater equality for all.

With intersectionality, for some, the tactic has been framing the concept as overzealous, even as having religious overtones. One conservative commentator said, "Intersectionality is becoming so influential that it haunts much of blue America in much the same way that Christian beliefs and cultures haunt the South. Even those who aren't full-on adherents have begun to adopt various intersectional habits, such as adjusting their language, deferring to experiential authority, and questioning the value of free speech."[4]

Others have simply dismissed it as "stupid."

The perceived imbalance of intersectionality is what seems to be at the root of its dissonant reception during its rise to superstardom over the past five or six years.

A core thesis of Crenshaw's work is that an increased focus on the most visible and vocal marginalizes groups of people who are multiply burdened and masks realities that cannot be understood as resulting from discrete cases of discrimination. It is easy to interpret the theory of intersectionality to be about individual experiences and as not being intricately aligned with the realities that are faced by oppressed groups because of their social standing. With a focus on individual experience, a critic can cleverly make their identity the central theme in their criticism, thus pointing at those who are anchored in the theory as being hostile and opposed to people of a particular identity who hold the most power, in solidarity with people who claim similar identities. The result is that intersectionality is often framed as a weapon against individuals—mostly white men—who consider themselves as the targets of "intersectional mobs."

I had an experience with a former employer that reminded me that I do not have racial privilege, although in many spaces I do have privilege of class and sexuality as a straight, heterosexual male. But I am Black, so my privilege has at least that line that it cannot cross.

As I stepped into the elevator on my way to a meeting in the executive suite of the building, I encountered a gentleman that I had seen for a few months walking about the company facilities but never had a chance to formally meet. His manager was a dear colleague who I had worked with and had a collegial relationship with. He was walking with an external vendor, and as we were making our way up to the same floor, I said hello. He didn't respond with a "hi" or "hello." He asked, "Can I see your badge?"

My immediate response was a bit of surprise, maybe even shock. And then a bit of confusion. After that, I calmed myself and said, "I'm sorry?" And he repeated himself, "Can I see your badge?" I pulled aside the coat covering my badge, smiled, and said, "I don't think we have met; I'm Amri."

I was a bit vexed. Reflecting later, my initial surprise waned. It reminded me of a scene in the late John Singleton's film *Higher Learning*, which was about racial tensions on a predominantly white college campus based in Southern California. In one scene, the campus security guards from the fictional Columbus University pull up at night to rappers Ice Cube's and Busta Rhymes's characters Fudge White and Dreads in an SUV. One of the officers says to them, "Can I see your ID?" Ice Cube calmly pulls out a flashlight of his own and says, "No, let us see your ID!" The officers mumble something under their breath and immediately move on.

If only I had been fast enough to use an Ice Cube line on him! What did happen was that as we were leaving the elevator, the company president greeted me by name and mentioned a meeting that was recently booked with me and my boss for later that week. I didn't gloat. Well, I did smile at the "campus security guard."

That situation didn't leave me irritated for long, but it was another reminder that my privilege didn't equate to advantage. Whether he was acting as a concerned corporate citizen when he asked to see my identification, or because I have melanated skin matters little. The fact that I had to question his rationale is what left me thoughtful. Why was it necessary for me to question his motivation?

After many readings of Crenshaw's original text and various interviews, it occurs to me that she is moving toward a similar goal of dismantling *oppressive and inequitable systems*. Her path to doing so was to use legal cases to show how multidimensionality and our lack of attention to it where race is concerned thwarts our efforts. What the coining of the term missed (as is often the case with new terminology) was taking a more in-depth approach to clearly look at how not all intersections occur equally in the systems in which we exist. The result has been an equivocation of distinctions—a lack of understanding, often unconscious notions held even by oppressed people, of how inequities occur differently due to the insidious nature of deeply ingrained structural artifacts. If honestly explored, such societal relics are almost impossible to avoid if you have worked, lived, read about, or breathed the air in most parts of the Westernized world.

Crenshaw's analysis of intersectionality without (originally) exploring the breadth of possible responses to it is not the "bad." The bad is that many people have not done a deeper level of exploration themselves. Professor Emerita Patricia Hill Collins, the first Black woman to serve as president of the American Sociology Association, offers that intersectional analysis was in play before the term was coined. And that while using Crenshaw's original article could be premature (especially as she has built a more robust theoretical foundation), the "amorphous and perhaps idiosyncratic sensibility" in how many well-meaning scholars and practitioners use it could also be shortsighted.[5] The concept of intersectionality when introduced was an evolution, and the idea continues to evolve. However, many consumers of the concept have not evolved with it.

Neither has it moved the conversation toward a space that challenges practitioners and those committed to equity to go beyond the individual impact into understanding how the systems in which we exist and operate are dictated by norms that are not universally recognized as disproportionally unfair. Many people talk about inequitable systems. Few act and consider the complexity of systemic defaults. These defaults create inequities that adversely impact everyone who has been part of any institution and organization touched by systems of oppression. If there are individuals or groups of people in your organization who are not able to thrive because of unfairness (or any form of dehumanization), the organization suffers—all stakeholders, directly or indirectly, are harmed. When developing an Inclusion System, we work to create the conditions for people to explore how the various dimensions of who they are and how they are treated intersect with those of others. Intersectionality has the potential to make this a reality. As it has been co-opted, that has not been the case.

The Ugly

If someone had asked me a few years ago, "How oppressed are you?" I would have been able to respond: "I'm Black, so theoretically and historically there is a level of oppression and subordination that I have been subjected to." At the same time, I have lived a life of privilege relative to most people in the world. And while I have wondered what life would be like if I had the network of privilege that some of my white friends have, it was never more than a thought experiment for my own reflection. I don't know if it was helpful. It basically resulted in me saying, "Of course I would definitely have more wealth. The data on that are clear," full stop.

Other than those brief moments in my mid-to-late thirties, I never explicitly considered my "level of oppression." It was not a thing to think about. That was until I spoke with a colleague who pointed me toward a website that allows one to select a variety of identities, starting with how much of a person of color you are or are not, all the way through to whether you are a devout Jew. When he first began describing it, I laughed hysterically because I thought he was making it up. Then he said, no, it really exists. So, I visited and have returned several times throughout my time doing research for this book. I'm still perplexed by the audacity of the inventors. And when I say audacity, I don't mean audacity in a profound way—more so like social media shorthand also known as "WTF."

The "Intersectionality Score Calculator" was not created by Kimberlé Crenshaw, any of her graduate students, or any other prominent intersectionality scholar. In fact, I am not sure who is responsible. There is no identifying information on the site. They are anonymous satirists who have added fuel to the DEI fire. [6]

The site describes intersectionality as "the theory that the overlap of various social identities, such as race, gender, and sexuality define your level of systemic oppression." And they go on to say, "but, [you] don't know how to compare your oppression with others. Now you can!"

Engaging with the site is an interesting experience. All of the thirteen original categories are on a sliding scale, meaning you can be somewhat gay, somewhat born outside of the UK/USA (or elsewhere, depending on your IP address), somewhat male or female, or somewhat between cis- and transgender. You can be somewhat rich or poor, a little younger or a lot older, and anywhere in between being very much and not at all able-bodied. English speaker privilege is assessed alongside one's declared religion, Christian, Muslim, and Jewish, of which you can be completely, some of, or none of each of them.

The creators claim that they "believe that people fit along a spectrum of identities. For example, you might be slightly bisexual, somewhat poor, Jewish but rarely wear a yarmulke, and native born but travel frequently abroad. By having this option to be 'somewhere in the middle,' this gives a more 'accurate' assessment of your intersectionality score."

While I am not sure I have all the combinations figured out, the creators claim that they calculate the scores by carefully considering "the factors that make up various forms of social pressure and oppression. Then, using multivariable analysis, we are able to calculate the contribution that each factor has on an individual relative to their demographic size." My conclusion is that they might see which groups are predominant groups in society based on their demographic research and score them on a continuum; but, more than likely, they simply made it up based on what they felt matched their intent to enrage, confuse, or delight site visitors and went with that. If I am correct about their intent, it is working.

Here are some comments from the site: "I've always considered myself a liberal, but this is disgusting." "You can give exclusive opportunities and promotions to people with high intersectionality scores so that they become more represented in positions of power." "You mean I should leave jobs empty and undone until a qualified person representing a smaller slice of humanity than average emerges?" "Can I use this calculator on others? *Yes!*" "Thanks for making it so easy for me to judge others!" "Having a high intersectionality score doesn't completely immunize you from being called an oppressor." "So I'm responsible for what other people call me and accuse me of? Seriously, fuck you guys." (The italics are comments from the site creators.)

A commenter from Ireland said, "I love it. Its condescending, patronising crap like this, dressed up in academic verbiage like a pig in makeup, which at last exposes the intellectual derangement of mainstream progressivism."

Another commenter, from Slovenia, added, "That's so inaccurate! I got lower scores for being transgender male than my transgender female friend, all other factors equal. Rubbish!" And one commenter from Sedalia, Missouri, stated what I think is the most accurate reflection: "For Entertainment Purposes Only."

People who consider themselves liberal are offended by the site. Those who are more conservative consider their position justified by the content. Other commenters simply found it weird. In all cases, the creators have met a goal of many who produce content in the age of social media: polarization and sensationalism.

What makes this website and its satirical posture fall into the "ugly" aspect of intersectionality is twofold. First, few people have really gone into the depths of what intersectionality is as a concept. This being the case, the nature of what the concept of intersectionality could serve as is lost to incompleteness like a stereotype. The information on the site is not altogether true or altogether false. This combination, as is the nature of satire, leaves people reflecting what is and what is not helpful to public discourse. In the case of the Intersectionality Score Calculator, if one is not aware of its satirical aim, it can easily be perceived as an attempt at a sort of truth. This is like what we discussed about meritocracy. Michael Young didn't want to inspire people to use meritocracy as a tool for the elites. In fact, his 1958 text was intended to do just the opposite—get British upwardly mobile middle- and upper-class subjects to see that their idea of fairness was equitable to themselves but was otherwise structured toward inequality for most. In most of our institutions, we have done the contrary of what Young fought his entire life to create: academic, social, and economic equity.

In the intentional or unintentional redefining of intersectionality through the experiences and stories emitted from the Intersectionality Score Calculator, we are left with something that becomes a bit sinister. You cannot blame the idea and you cannot excuse it. You can't say it is "wrong" and you cannot condone it as something universally instructive.

Intersectionality can teach us about the complexity of humankind and our interactions. The Intersectionality Score Calculator tries to lazily simplify the concept and the space it creates for exploration of multidimensionality. That's what makes it ugly. There is an urgent need to expand the space for diversity's complex nature; this satire, intentionally or unintentionally, shrinks it. Or does it?

That brings us to the second reason the score calculator shows us the ugly side of intersectionality: it holds up a mirror to our usage, weaponization, and misappropriation of the exclusive lexicon. We have not been fully responsible with intersectionality as scholars and practitioners, or as social justice activists using the term. In fact, it was easy to be arrogant with intersectionality. Professor Crenshaw used examples of legal decisions to non-exhaustively illustrate some dynamics of a Black woman's intersectional nature. Some have taken this to mean that it is all about Black women or queer Black women. As Professor Patricia Hill Collins says, intersectionality has "definitional dilemmas." But although the exploration of the intersection of sex, race, and gender is critical to creating organizational equity, intersectionality is not *exclusively* for that purpose.

Some DEI practitioners zoom in *or* out. Urgency of the moment, a limiting context, or what is considered most important as a reflection of an individual's identity is prioritized. Others take the path of the reflective practitioner, as described by Professor Donald Schön.[7] The reflective practitioner doesn't simply depend on their experience, they deliberately reflect on their experience and that of those they are in co-creation with. This is essential and moves one from a perspective of zooming in *or* out to one of zooming in *and* out. The difference is minor. Distinctions in how it shows up when scaled beyond the individual are significant.

We Create Intersectionality as Good

Conversely, the good that we can absolutely build on from intersectionality is something to be encouraged by and excited about. The good of intersectionality is the capacity and reflexivity of being able to zoom in and out of contexts. It's important that we "zoom in" and look at various contexts closely, such as the lived experiences of people who strongly identify with one group, like Black people. We can "zoom out" to see that there is profound overlapping and similarity of attributes across our collective humanity.

Making DEI actionable and sustainable means that it first must be accessible to everyone. Intersectionality can serve as a tool to go beyond the simplified ways that organizations tend to categorize distinctions.

We can use intersectionality as a vehicle for all to see ourselves and the complexity of our various dimensions as complement. All combinations of identity make up what we call [organizational, micro, and macro] culture. Intersectionality can serve our organization as a critical tool for reflection, enhancing our capacity to move into, outside of, around, and through organizational contexts without getting stuck in any one—or two—fixed positions.

We have this gift, but it is important that, in this case, we "look a gift horse in the mouth," so to speak. That is, while making meaning of intersectionality, we cannot create a vacuum or a silo that prevents or, even worse, weaponizes the concept because we use it to further an exclusive agenda. Rather, we must use the idea to think about and ask the right questions of ourselves related to our agendas. Meaning, we have to explore and make sense with those who have tendencies to zoom in or out of places we don't zoom into and see our organization in ways we might not be able to in creating equitable outcomes for everyone.

—Sincerely, Your CEO

This CEO recognizes that we have not consistently opened our own spaces to allow for thoughtful criticism to be the standard as we evolve our practical understanding of intersectionality and adopt practices to make it revolutionary rather than dichotomous and dull—the mirror image of its opposite intent.

Intersectionality offers a conceptual space to explore the burgeoning multidimensionality in organizational life. It can expand the space to explore complexity, but that is not what it has consistently done. Crenshaw is interested in making room for more advocacy and what she calls "remedial practices." I would refer to it as designing organizations for systemic equity.

We need a purer dose of intersectionality. That means we need to extract its essence. How do we best serve it through our conceptions and actions? And how does it best serve us as a tool to refine our lenses and expand our apertures?

Context drives content. If the context remains limited, we will lose intersectionality and all its power to the "ugly." I would argue that it has already happened to some extent, and there will be some YouTube stars, bloggers, and politically-oriented public intellectuals from across political spectra, out of convenience and in deference to their brands, who hold on to their points of view without consideration of the various contexts that are always at play. Their perspectives should be both welcomed and criticized, not with the fire of annihilation, but with a light of humility. A light appropriately intensified but always with the intention of enlightening us as practitioners to be vigilant perspective takers, diligent with our inquiry, thoughtful with our actions, and mindful that there is always more "there" than we can quickly or independently understand.

Years ago, while building employee resource groups across the globe with clients and then with my former employer, I had a theoretical position that I saw as reflective of intersectionality and multidimensionality. I didn't believe in single-identity ERGs. That is, I felt that if any ERG was to get financial support, it had to be inclusive of people who may not be historically considered from a particular identity group. For example, a women's ERG needed to intentionally have men as part of it. I saw and see ERGs as spaces to lay the groundwork for greater solidarity across identities.

I wrote a blog about it in 2009 that didn't have the most favorable response from all practitioners, as they were intent on saying that these groups created "safe spaces" for the members. I didn't disagree that the spaces were safe and needed to be. But I felt that the spaces needed to be and could be safe even for people from groups who didn't "match" the identity of the majority—e.g., men having a safe place in a women's ERG.

My sense remains that if an organization is aspiring to be inclusive as a default or normative way of being, ERGs could be bridges between values and backgrounds as Inclusion Systems are developed with the intention of elevating the superset of humanity in its entirety.

Intersectionality, when framed as a container to look at organizational life with a multidimensional lens, is characterized by two fundamental elements of an Inclusion System: *interdependence* and *mindful reflection*. Interdependence in this sense goes beyond interpersonal inclusion. It also includes systems interacting with each other. It speaks to the reality that everyone and everything in our organizations rely on one another in explicit and implicit ways. All contributions and the context of each contributor are vital to overall organizational function. Intersectionality allows us to see these multiple dimensions as more than the sum of their parts—each connecting with the other, like particles combining to create molecules.

Mindful reflection, as it relates to intersectionality, means that the perspectives of these differences and similarities are required if we want to create inclusion as aligned with purpose and that is therefore sustainable.

Our values are on a continuum, often much closer to one another than we realize. A more complete construction of intersectionality holds a space for us to inquire with greater depth. With this depth is a wellspring of potential to inspire the extraordinary—consistently considering the whole rather than narrowly anchoring on our myriad indivisible parts.

Overstanding Exclusion

"A man's social self is the recognition which he gets from his mates. We are not only gregarious animals, liking to be in sight of our fellows, but we have an innate propensity to get ourselves noticed, and noticed favorably, by our kind. No more fiendish punishment could be devised, were such a thing physically possible, than that one should be turned loose in society and remain absolutely unnoticed by all the members thereof.

If no one turned around when we entered, answered when we spoke, or minded what we did, but if every person we met 'cut us dead,' and acted as if we were non-existing things, a kind of rage and impotent despair would ere long well up in us, from which the cruelest bodily tortures would be a relief; for these would make us feel that however bad might be our plight, we had not sunk to such a depth as to be unworthy of attention at all."[1]

—William James, 1890

"Because it is not what we say to each other every day that established all the meaning and beauty and truth our everyday conversations contain; it is everything we think before we speak."

—Tor Nørretranders (*The User Illusion*, 1991)

As a field, DEI has been largely focused on what organizations should do in order to embrace diversity, create equity, and foster inclusion. Although the initial priority was mitigating discriminatory practices in the workplace, the bulk of early efforts were reactive. Contemporary approaches haven't changed dramatically from where things started. When individual discrimination showed its face, those responsible for employee relations, diversity, or for adherence to US Equal Employment Opportunity laws (EEO) would react to the individual's claim and decide whether what was done was right or wrong within the organizational code of conduct and the laws of the land.

The result of most of these examinations (all in the US) would find an individual or class situation that could be considered a misunderstanding. They would be dismissed, with the majority having an inconclusive finding. The reasons for this could have been that federal employment discrimination laws didn't cover the complaint, or that the incident fell outside of the statute of limitations, or the employer was not of sufficient size to be investigated to validate the claim. In a 2018 UK study with more than five thousand BME (Black, Minority, and Ethnic) worker responses, 70 percent of Asians and Blacks reported that they had experienced racial harassment at work within the past five years. The report also found that more than half of those who reported experiencing racism at work experienced adverse mental health impacts. Several also said racism affected their physical health, resulting in them taking a period of sick leave.[2]

These data are, at best, minimally reflective of the discrimination and systemic exclusion in organizations and institutions around the world. They don't even include discrimination related to religion, sexual orientation, caste and social status, or a surplus of other domains where historically subordinated groups are victims of economic, social, or physical injustices. The problems are pervasive and require diligence to address them and their adverse impact on individuals, families, organizations, and the communities that people and organizations call home.

Many factors perpetuate social exclusion. And, as with any societal phenomenon, there are many stakeholders who must examine the root causes and move closer to sustainable approaches to mitigate unnecessary suffering. One challenge is that when the data are crunched and presented as one group of people doing poorly and the other excelling, or maintaining the historically established status quo, a binary conclusion, an "us vs. them" discourse, is usually the outcome. This social phenomenon, reinforced by current technologies and ideologies, persists over time and is grossly oversimplified and incomplete. Directly or indirectly, discrimination negatively impacts everyone.

Discrimination and Ostracism

Discrimination and exclusion are often used synonymously, particularly when discussing diversity, equity, and inclusion in organizations. For those who are more legally oriented, discrimination has a close relationship with exclusion, but the potential course of legal action behind it is much clearer.

Discrimination is defined as either a "distinction among things" or "to treat someone as worse than others."[3] In the latter sense, *discrimination* prevents people, for reasons of their identity, from sharing as full partners the rights and benefits guaranteed to other members of society. For definitional purposes, then, I argue that *discrimination* is linked to the notion of *inferiority*. In *discriminatory practices*, a status of *inferiority* is assigned to the "other," making their difference the mark of such inferiority.

Discrimination can take a variety of forms. Let's explore a few.

Sexual harassment. Whether it is an unwelcome or offensive comment, physical advance, or request (even jokingly) for sexual favors, such behavior is the most common form of workplace discrimination. Despite the global #MeToo movement, there are still many people who choose not to report such acts of misconduct out of fear of retaliation. Often, these retaliatory behaviors can be easily masked to create the perception of them being benign oversights.

Ageism. Globally, age-oriented discrimination is growing quickly. According to the Office of the United Nations High Commissioner for Human Rights, more than one in five of the world's people will be sixty or older by 2050. And with the population having more older people and needs beyond what family members can provide, the need for employment grows. Despite many people over sixty being in excellent health, age-related discrimination persists.

Racial discrimination. The history of racial discrimination has been detailed in depth, especially in 2020, as a confluence of discrimination in healthcare and police violence against Black people that has been brought to the fore by COVID-19 and a variety of incidents of Black people being killed by police officers in the United States. Racial harassment in the workforce can be difficult to clarify.

What's more likely is for someone to experience a form of discrimination that is much more subtle. *Micro-inequities* occur whenever people are perceived as different from the majority in an environment. Mary Rowe, a professor at the MIT Sloan School of Management, describes them as "small events which are often ephemeral and hard-to-prove, events which are covert, often unintentional, frequently unrecognized by the perpetrator."[4]

Disability discrimination. When people experience disability discrimination, they are unfavorably treated because of a physical or mental impairment that substantially influences their major life activities like walking, talking, seeing, learning, and socializing, but not limited to these components alone.

Discrimination because of one's disablement is one of the most reported and widespread forms of harassment. A lot of disability discrimination is related to assumptions made by decision-makers who are uninformed or underinformed about abilities and how choices on shallow understanding led to discriminatory practices.

Sexual orientation and gender identity discrimination. Outside of the US and western Europe, people are far less tolerant of homosexuality, and it plays a role in the workplace. Much of the discriminatory attitude about people who identify as LGBTQA+ stems from religiosity. The acceptance of homosexuality also correlates with per capita income. Countries with the highest per-capita gross domestic product—more than 50,000 USD—have the highest acceptance of non-heterosexuals. Countries with GDP less than 10,000 USD have the lowest.

Discrimination happens globally, but the reporting of it is dependent on either local and national laws or global company policies that offer protections that not all nation-states mirror in their national laws.[5] In the US and most western European countries, there are anti-discrimination policies that encompass people identifying as gay, lesbian, and transgender. However, it is important to recognize that these policies are not necessarily long-standing. In the US, it was only as of June 15, 2020, that the Supreme Court ruled that the Civil Rights Act of 1964 protects employees from discrimination based on sexual orientation or gender identity. Globally, only seventy-seven countries prohibit discrimination in employment because of sexual orientation. Exclusion, in contrast to discrimination, is defined as "to expel or to keep out" and as a condition of "incompatibility."[6]

Maria Mercedes Gomez states, "If what characterizes exclusion is incompatibility, then the practices that operate to expel 'material or immaterial objects' from a determinate system might be called exclusionary practices."[7] She continues to say that exclusionary practices aren't intended to frame the other as inferior, which was the rationale for *Brown v. Board of Education* (1954).

Many institutions have fostered largely covert practices that create out-groups but at the same time de-emphasize difference to the point of invisibility. We still have many "invisible" people, those who feel as though they must hide a part of their humanity, inside of our organizations. This sad reality forces those who identify in the out-group to assimilate or be metaphorically (Kenji Yoshino calls it "covering")[8] or physically removed. In some cases, corporate policies such as performance management, talent acquisition, and talent development force or filter out those who are not well versed in the behavioral strategies of the majority power holders. Conversely, some who may even have been exposed and are able to navigate an organizational cultural terrain built on a foundation of exclusion-oriented operating ways might opt to remove themselves.

What happens, in addition to what Gomez states, is that the process of "erasing the other from the system" is often coupled with the closing off of opportunities, access, and hope. One may use the medical term *occlusion* in this case. In pathology, this would constitute "a complete obstruction of the breath passage in the articulation of a speech sound."

Many times, when people experiencing exclusion have shared their story with me, they have referred to feeling "blocked," that "*they* are getting in the way of [my idea]," or that someone is "getting in between me and the [decision-maker(s)]" and a variety of other metaphors related to the closing off of possibilities through a dominant group's (or individual's) occlusion of others with less power.

I have seen more and more DEI practitioners increase their focus on inclusion. Their work has been about behavioral change and organizational maturity in the space, along with structural ways of being inclusive. More recently, advancing behavioral and structural inclusion has been manifesting through anti-racism efforts and calls to address a long-standing history of global racism. This is understandable and needed. We should absolutely focus on what we would like to manifest in organizational culture, particularly inclusion.

Yet, we have barely deepened our understanding of what is generally perceived as inclusion's counterforce, exclusion. Is it possible that being focused on inclusion without having a deeper understanding of exclusion is shortsighted? Many consider the terms we use to be interchangeable, yet for someone who is well-versed in constructs like ostracism, discrimination, inequity, and social exclusion, these terms are not direct synonyms for "exclusion" as we so often perceive it when working on DEI in organizational life. Like most things, it is considerably more complex. And in many ways, it is much more insidious than the common opposite-of-inclusion framing that organizations can be heavily focused on.

Discrimination has legal consequences. Yet, proving that the behavior and actions of another are illegally discriminatory is difficult. The burden of proof lies with the victims, and the legal precedent is not in their favor. For many, one internal reporting channel is employee relations, a function that most large and mid-sized organizations have. In smaller companies, the process usually runs through a senior human resource professional or office tasked with mediating between a senior and junior employee regarding what is generally miscommunication that escalates because of the incongruent contexts (at times toxic or sinister, but rarely) of the parties involved.

Like formal discrimination complaints (e.g., to the US Equal Employment Opportunity Commission), most employee relations cases end without any action that benefits those who file. This means that based on the reviewers' findings and the parameters that necessitate legal action, the complaint didn't contain enough evidence for the alleged perpetrator to be held accountable. The result of many of the cases is profound disappointment and often disillusionment for the complainant. This can lead to everything from disengagement and diminishing job performance to (voluntary or involuntary) separation.

While the company often gets away without any immediate consequences, those filing the complaints end up being hurt for doing the right thing. And although retaliation is illegal and against most companies' codes of conduct, it still happens in mostly covert ways. So, when companies say that they would like people to "speak up," the reality is that the probability of extrinsic adversity for someone who does speak up may be higher than if they would have chosen to stay silent. The data indicate that coming forth and sharing one's truth, at least on the individual level, is disadvantageous in the long term.[9]

Lawmakers around the world typically didn't write discrimination laws to help employees. While many politicians have been influenced by activists like Cesar Chavez, Mary Harris "Mother" Jones, A. Philip Randolph, and others when running for reelection, their efforts have been far from balanced in the interests of workers. In the US, workplace law is relatively weak and is limited by reach, capacity, and accountability.

For example, the Equal Employment Opportunity Commission (EEOC), created under Title VII of the Civil Rights Act of 1964, could not sue employers on behalf of employees until 1972. Even then, the EEOC's capacity to do so was restricted by staffing and the burden of proof. By law, the EEOC must show *explicit proof* of discriminatory acts. This requires the EEOC to investigate claims, which can take up to six months. Prior to that, they must determine if the cases are strong enough for an investigation to start. And, even when that is determined, 82 percent of cases don't receive any form of relief such as monetary compensation or accommodations (e.g., for a worker who uses a wheelchair). Of all cases investigated, less than 2 percent find clear evidence of discrimination by law when related to age, sex, disability, race, or retaliation.

Something that could subjectively be reported as discriminatory may not be assessed as such by an employer. Thus, because of limited restorative outcomes, the punitive consequences for individuals don't necessarily prevent people from discriminating. This is the case even in the present day, and not just in the US.[10]

While exclusion can serve as a broad term for many types of actions and behaviors, our notion of it doesn't allow us to address workplace dynamics in the most effective manner. Managing something like discrimination in many cases may not be the best path forward. Whether that be through external legal and regulatory entities of governments or via internal mechanisms, there is a significant and likely unreachable distance between reporting and resolving discrimination cases. And the incentives occur as seemingly more favorable when organizations can excuse themselves from accountability. The perception of potential gains for being vigilant for fairness and encouraging people to acknowledge and address issues that have a negative individual or systemic impact (i.e., equity) can strike one as very unfavorable compared to the probable risks.

Most companies have yet to reach a point where they are prepared to openly acknowledge that adverse behavioral, structural, and systemic dynamics in their organizations may require more vigilance and accountability to prevent harm. Conversely, firms might be motivated toward more actionable and sustainable ways of response if they reflected on the inhumanity and insidiousness of a more focused set of behaviors, such as ostracism, instead of a simplified interpretation of exclusion.

Ostracism is "exclusion by general consent from common privileges or social acceptance."[11] Ostracism is a form of exclusion. To me, it is one of the most dehumanizing forms of social exclusion. I say this because, although it falls into the category of exclusion, it goes beyond simply being left out. It is a form of manipulation that seeks to control or reprogram someone to assimilate, conform, or suffer. Conform *or* be devalued or degraded to such an extent that the possibility of meaningful connection with an in-group is no longer an option. Even if the ostracized person submits to the manipulation, there is no guarantee that the ostracizers will accept the surrender.

People, often those with power or influence, choose ostracism for two reasons. First, it works. And second, you can get away with it. It's almost impossible to make a case that someone has been lying (usually by omission) if they ignore you. And if you were to confront that person about their behavior, they could easily deny it. Unlike verbal or written insults or threatening physical gestures, ostracism is primarily invisible. The victim has little to no evidence that they can document. Ostracism is often part of a persistent and progressive campaign to diminish an individual's value and presence in the workplace.

Anyone who has experienced ostracism knows how soul-crushing it is. It is a spirit assassin. If you are the unfortunate target of this behavior and complain or point out other workplace problems, the bully is usually exceptionally skilled at making it appear as if you are the cause. Other employees will potentially hesitate in contacting you except when compulsory by business or social norms. Your efforts to comment in meetings are interrupted or spoken over. Your thoughts or comments passively dismissed.[12]

Nothing is beneficial about ostracism. There are times when victims move toward pro-social (try to connect and integrate more with colleagues) versus anti-social behaviors (become avoidant, minimally interacting with colleagues) because of their experience. Kipling Williams is a distinguished professor in the Department of Psychological Sciences at Purdue University. He is most noted for his leading research on ostracism. Williams's Temporal Need-Threat Model in Figure 3 shows how exposure to ostracism produces similar initial impact to everyone.[13]

Initially, the response, in what Williams calls the Reflexive Stage, is pain. This finding confirms the results of experience done with a simulated ball toss game called Cyberball.

Williams and his study team created Cyberball. Participants in a ball toss video game were either included or ostracized. After logging on, players

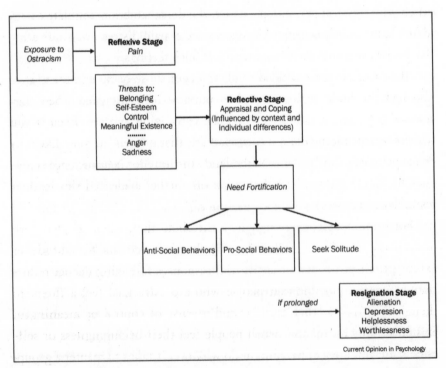

Figure 3

were pitted against two other players. In reality, the players were icons that either threw the ball to the participants or skipped them and only threw to each other. Participants were included in five degrees, ranging from overinclusion to complete ostracism. The study found that the higher the degree of ostracism, the more demoralized and deflated the participants felt as their belongingness and self-esteem diminished.[14]

Williams's Temporal Need-Threat Model and his research with the Cyberball game illustrate that, minimally, ostracism causes psychological and emotional pain. University of California professors Matthew Lieberman and Naomi Eisenberger, alongside Williams, devised a set of neuroimaging experiments using Cyberball showing that it also causes physical pain.

The researchers took Williams's Cyberball game and connected participants to an fMRI scanner. When the computer stopped throwing the ball to a participant's icon, the scanner showed that the brain region associated with physical pain lit up. In fact, the dorsal anterior cingulate cortex (dACC), previously linked to the experience of pain distress, was indicating that social exclusion hurts more than just one's feelings.[15]

Their experiment extended to observers of those being excluded. They also had the brain region related to physical pain triggered when they *watched* the computer program simulate ostracizing another. Even if you witness ostracism, the brain is so empathetic that it "feels" it, too—like how one experiences similar pain. Netherlands Institute for Neuroscience scholars Christian Keysers and Valeria Gazzola further evidenced this in their research describing the brain as "vicarious."[16]

For some people, there may be a threshold that, when coupled with one's lived experience, influences whether one retreats to solitude or exhibits their pro-social or anti-social responses following deeper reflection. It is even possible that people who are ostracized feel a threat to their belongingness that goes beyond a sense of control or meaningful existence. This means that when people feel their belongingness or self-esteem are threatened, they might do whatever it takes to reenter a group. They do so without any delusions about being able to "fit in" with the ostracizers. Their tactic could become subversion for self-preservation. "Keep your enemies closer."

Considering the above, think about what happens when an ostracized person remains on a team. For example, imagine the mental health impacts of ostracism and consider what might be one's strategy to stay relevant.

If an ostracized victim has a robust social network, they could retreat to their sense of belonging and embeddedness within it. If they don't have such a network, they could have other mechanisms (e.g., a constellation of mentors) that provide a vector for social-psychological sustenance. Without some aspect of either of these support mechanisms, the toll on a person could result in harm (to the individual and organization), anti-social behaviors, and movement to the resignation stage of Williams's model. If you have ever heard of the phrase "quit and stays," consider that people who are ostracized can easily move into such a role whereby they cease to care about their performance. Their goal is to survive (with a paycheck) until another opportunity is secured elsewhere.

Given the overwhelmingly negative potential consequences of ostracism to employees and their communities, to what level do organizations need to take preventative measures or address it anytime it occurs?

Occlusion and Agency

A significant amount of my leadership coaching and mentorship over the past fifteen years has been with senior and junior emerging executives and managers. Many of them have been women, and several were women of color. All of them were hardworking, committed, and ambitious. Most had consistently excelled, but for some reason, did not feel as if they were advancing and making the impact that they aspired to.

At issue for most was whether they could influence those in power in a way that allowed them to make the impact they felt capable of. Many struggled with the belief that they could manifest the impact they envisioned making. It was certainly not because of a lack of capability. My clients and mentees have been among the brightest people I have ever met. I learned and continue to learn from each of them. Capability was never the problem.

The problem was agency.

The concept of agency has been long examined in the social sciences and overlaps with various notions of human engagement and interaction. Albert Bandura, in developing his seminal work on social cognitive theory, claims that one's agency comes via the accumulation of knowledge through the observation of others via social engagement, experiences, and other external media.[17]

At the heart of social cognitive theory lies two concepts—human capability and human agency. Human capability speaks to the evolution of one's capacity to acquire knowledge and skills directly and implicitly. In organizational systems, building capabilities through experiences, relationships, goal setting, and constant expansions of one's ability to contribute through information extracted from various networks is implicitly expected. The more a person characteristically develops a record of dynamic capability, the more they can be rewarded through work and roles with greater responsibility and control.

Conversely, an individual's sense of agency embodies the belief that we can sufficiently control our capability development. It doesn't mean that we believe or desire to do this on our own. The more robust agency we possess, the more confidence we have in our ability to adapt and evolve in exercising our influence. Agency is the self-confidence that we can perform independently and interdependently while navigating the various circumstances that inevitably emerge in the process of conducting business.

Having a greater sense of agency would likely translate into more work effort. I support research showing that people who have a sense of autonomy have more robust employee engagement.

Most stellar performers that I have encountered are given or demand the autonomy to dig into their work, have a sense of control about how they can go about creating impact, and receive reinforcement that those they work with value and appreciate their contributions. Conversely, I have also encountered high performers who feel like they are constantly monitored for mistakes and rarely receive positive feedback. If they get feedback from supervisors or senior leaders, it's not affirmative and developmental. Instead, it's vague and filled with ambiguity.

What binds this latter group of high performers, some being women and people with identities underrepresented in their organization, is a sense that somehow, after all their hard work, they feel excluded—or, more accurately, *occluded*. They are good at what they do. They get affirmation from peers and colleagues that reflects their expectations of exceeding performance. Yet, from those who have the most significant influence on their next steps inside the firm and thus their careers, they feel unseen.

However, these long-suffering high performers also encounter a paradox. If their superiors or peers have negatively impacted their sense of confidence and have influence, they may worry about moving out of the organization. In their current organization, they are still valued for their technical proficiency. Yet, suppose they have come to doubt their ability to relate and influence critical decisions and have influence with their bosses. In that case, their mindset and lower sense of agency can negatively impact their contributions.

Given the complexity of human relationships and sentiments, we cannot conclude that those who feel excluded are simply the victims of bad managers or an endemically non-inclusive organizational culture. However, we can conclude that if a person doesn't feel included and has ample core features of human agency as described by Bandura, self-exclusion is more likely. Good employees always have options.

In a case such as this, exclusion results in an (often) undocumented adverse consequence for an organization. Exclusion's impact is not simply reflective of harm to the victim. Exclusion is more complicated than that. We can never know the context of each situation in its entirety. What we might call out as exclusion functioning as ostracism or occlusion—that is, any dynamic involving the lack of creating space for the so-called other—might not be what we think it is. It might simply be the result of differences in our respective contexts.

Exformation: What If We Have a Different Framing for Exclusion?

My father, Larry D. Johnson Sr., was my first hero. Well, maybe my brother, Larry Jr., and my dad captured that space simultaneously. Nonetheless, I soaked everything up from them that I could. Where my father was concerned, this came down to the way he walked, talked (think James Earl Jones combined with the actor Richard Roundtree's character in the 1970s *Shaft* films), and especially his facial expressions in different situations—from his Muhammad Ali–like animated expression of opening his eyes when saying something humorously or provocatively to his slightly furrowed brow that left a distinct line in his forehead perpendicular to his eyebrows when he was thinking through something, whether he was listening or sharing something he was focused on. I mimicked his actions, tone of voice, and facial expressions.

Little did I know, I would unwittingly mirror him until this day. My father's brothers and sister all have variations on our furrowed brow facial expression. My brother often had it. My niece is now twenty-two years old and has been making the expression since she was very young. Most recently, my son (at as early as six months of age) makes the same facial expression when presented with new data (which is pretty much all of the time). We could see him make the expression at two months, and when my twin stepchildren first observed it, the girl twin, Romy, coined the phrase "Johnson Blick." *Blick* is a German word equivalent to "look" or "expression."

So, my son Kai, like his grandfather, great-uncles and -aunts, uncle, father, and cousin, exhibits the Johnson Blick in situations where he is processing something. Kai never has had the chance to know his grandfather or uncles (except for his youngest great-uncle a few times), and he occasionally sees his cousin on camera. He sees me, but given the acuity of a newborn's

vision, it is hard to say if the Johnson Blick is nurture, nature, or some combination of the two. In any scenario, it doesn't matter. If you are a Johnson
(or maybe even a descendent of my paternal grandmother, whose maiden
name was Jackson), as Prince said, "you've got the look."[18]

Now, go back in time to me sitting in a restaurant in Cambridge, Massachusetts. I was there with a member of the executive leadership team of
my employer. He was (and still is) someone I have a lot of respect for and was
excited when he was assigned as my mentor as part of a formal mentoring
program for so-called high-potential employees. As we enjoyed our meal,
he asked me about my thoughts related to our organizational culture and
its evolution. I cannot recall everything I said, but I remember that part of
the response included a personal story. In telling the story, I was thinking
deeply about how it occurred to me, and while speaking I reflexively had the
Johnson Blick.

When I finished speaking, my colleague said, not commenting on the
story I just told or my thoughts about the evolution of organizational culture, "Wow, that look you had on your face was so scary!" Hearing that
response for the first time, if you are a DEI practitioner, you might frame
it as a microaggression, and you would be correct. You may even have said
that it was racist because a white man said this to me. Right now, given the
global tenor of the conversation about race and racial justice, you might have
a motivation to call this leader out and/or at the least make sure you educated him on the impact that such a statement might have had on me and
could have on others. It would be appropriate to do so.

Yet, none of the above came to mind. I was not offended. I didn't consider that he said what he did because of my size (he happens to be shorter
and smaller in stature than me as most people in the world are), or my voice
resonating at a relatively low octave, or because I am Black. None of those
things occurred to me. Did I like that after sharing all of what I shared that
that was his initial response? I looked at him a bit puzzled (with what I recall
was a slightly less-intense Johnson Blick). He then responded to what I said,
and we had a robust discussion about it.

My puzzled look in response to my colleague's behavior was not excusing him from doing something that could be considered harmful to another person, with or without my descriptors. If I was more sensitive about how I look or hadn't felt listened to in the past, I may have felt different than I did. In retrospect, I don't condone his behavior. But I don't condemn him for his past actions either.

What I would do now or would have done if I had seen or heard of him responding to others like this would likely be much different than how I responded directly. And, I imagine, knowing him to be quite attuned to the sentiments of others and current societal contexts, he would be much more mindful of his statements. I don't think he would say it.

When we started our mentoring relationship, I had been at the company for one or two years. We semi-frequently engaged and were collegial, yet we didn't know each other as well as we do now. He had the chance to see the Johnson Blick on many occasions, frequently along with my one-eyebrow raised Dr. Spock Blick. He now knows me with much richer context and nuance. And similarly, I know him better, too.

If he did happen to make a statement like that to me, I would sincerely ask about his intention. I would do so with humility and care, and perhaps a bit of humor. Our cultivated context would extend dialogue and learning that we have engaged in for many years. The result would be a deeper relational capacity and a better understanding of how to mitigate potentially subtle acts of exclusion.

As we got to know each other better, we fine-tuned how we related to one another. Because we found a lot of value in our relationship, we learned how to read one another's gestures and take one another's words. We developed a shorthand when we spoke. Our conversations were meaningful not simply because of what stories or ideas we exchanged or what we said, but because of all the (unsaid) things we discarded. Our *exformation* played a bigger role than the information exchanged.

Exformation is a term coined by Tor Nørretranders, a Danish journalist and author, in his 1991 book, *The User Illusion*. Nørretranders's book explored consciousness as an idea. While a lot of learning in organizations has been about unconsciousness for the past several years, Nørretranders questioned the notion of consciousness. A data point often used in unconscious bias training comes from Nørretranders. He concluded, "The flow of information, measured in bits per second is described as the *bandwidth of capacity* of consciousness. The bandwidth of consciousness is far lower than the bandwidth of our sensory receptors." Nørretranders questions the significance and relevance of the phenomena of consciousness.[19]

Nørretranders's book title comes from a term coined by computer scientists at the Xerox Palo Alto Research Center based in Palo Alto, California. Scientists determined that it doesn't matter if someone using a computer knows how it works. Users want to use computers as tools to meet their objectives.

The "user illusion" is why software programmers, app developers, website architects, and marketers spend a considerable amount of time iterating and improving on the user interface or UI of their digital product or product consumed with digital tools. UI, as it has evolved, has expanded to UX or the overall user experience. Those in the UI/UX space generally are not doing their job to help users of their products, services, and interfaces understand what goes *into* creating what they deliver. They do what they must to make sure the user gets what they need *out of* the creation.

There's clarity (often on both sides) that the depth of what goes into a creation is far vaster than what comes out of it. Let's use the example of a video game. Gamers may know that a great amount of sophisticated code is on the game's insides. Some may care. Most only care about the experience of playing against their friends, colleagues, and competitors around the world.

They are concerned about perception, and that is the essence of consciousness—perception is where consciousness lives. The user illusion makes it clear that perception is a sort of incomplete reality. In most cases, individuals take what they need, and no further "reality" is necessary. The illusion is sufficient. While diplomatic about the man/machine metaphors that have been historically promoted (i.e., brain as steam engine, then switchboard, and more recently computer), Nørretranders equates the user illusion with consciousness.

He states, "Our consciousness is our user illusion for ourselves and the world. . . . The user illusion is one's very own map of oneself and one's possibilities of intervening in the world."[20] The second sentence above makes consciousness sound a lot like agency. Does consciousness give us a sense of control or lack thereof? Or is the iteration of eleven million bits per second of information that needs to be discarded to conclude how one's level of control or sense of agency occurs to oneself?

It's the discarded information, or *exformation*, that I find most relevant to how we view exclusion. Nørretranders says that our interpretation of information is closer to exformation. "Exformation is what is [excluded] en route, before expression." It is about the mental processing that we do to make what we say meaningful. It is all the information in our heads that we discard to make sense. This is not always the case because, as the author states, "We have no idea of the exformation in most of the messages we hear. We guess, sense, and support—but we do not know."

We can't know the exformation of every interaction. However, as shown in the example about my colleague and his reaction to my facial expression, if I didn't have certain exformation about him and his intentions, I would have reacted in a way that might have led our relationship to never go beyond that mentoring lunch. I more than likely would have filed him away as being oriented in a particular manner. An incomplete context would have framed my interactions with him and those who reported to him.

Our framing for exclusion can be different. What seems like acts of exclusion could simply be, and probably often are, that we have disparate exformation. Nørretranders says that information is perpendicular to exformation. That means that if exformation is happening much more prolifically than where the two intersect, the probability of missing meaning is higher than the chance of making meaning.

Let's say you are in a meeting with a total of eight people, including yourself. You are leading and facilitating the meeting about a project that is moving into its final phase. While you have worked with five of the people in the meeting quite a bit throughout this eighteen-month project, three are new and have specific expertise needed for this phase. This is the fifth weekly meeting with the new and older team members.

Everyone has access to communications and files since the project's inception via the collaboration platform. In essence, much of the *information* is there for their consumption. The three new members shared before the first meeting with you that they were up to speed on the project plan and have read what comes next. During the meeting, you are excited as usual, articulating the critical nature of the current phase and the necessity to make sure all moves fluidly forward.

You set critical tasks to be done, primarily by the new team members, given their expertise being most relevant at present. A few days later, when expecting feedback from the new team members, they don't come to you when expected and you're slightly annoyed as a result. To assure that you were clear about your requests, you reach out to the team members you have been working with for a while and ask them if what you said was clear. Two of them confirm that what you asked for was unambiguous. You quietly feel like your exasperation is justified.

Subsequently, you have a meeting with a colleague who goes on and on about the level of work and detail your new team members are putting into the project. She shares how energized they are by you and how much they appreciate the autonomy you have given them to make decisions and drive things forward.

What they didn't know is how you prefer an iterative approach to design and implementation. While you were taking in your colleague's comments, longer-term members on the team had gone to their newer colleagues to give them insight that you needed more frequent updates. The new team members were surprised. You never explicitly signaled to them that this was the case.

From that point on, they started to spend more time with you each week. This resulted in greater clarity about what allowed them to do their best work, and in them understanding that you like initiative and also want to learn together as much as possible. The project moved forward brilliantly, and the team jelled due to more time spent and an evolved context or *exformation*.

This is a relatively benign example and a happy outcome. If you hadn't attentively listened to your colleague or the team hadn't been so helpful with one another, the result could have been different. The opposite happens quite often. People don't default to helping behaviors and sense-making unless team culture and structure have been fostered as enablers. Many times, the result is that those not "in the know" are left feeling perplexed and, in too many cases, like they don't fit in. Combine this with a history of exclusionary acts toward marginalized communities and you have what occurs to people as an "ism." The reality is, while one's identity might reinforce historical pain because of disparate context, the negative impacts are universal. Think distrust, fear, confusion, hesitation, and any sentiment that is contrary to people thriving and your culture being generative along with project missteps (an outcome of the above).

How do we recognize when we have common or disparate exformation?

Consider exformation like an infinite virtual line that travels perpendicularly through a horizontal plane the surface of which is the information you deem as interesting in a message you send (Figure 4). Where the two meet is the point at which a message is conveyed. Can you see how easy it is to have disparate exformation? For sure you will engage with people who have higher levels of common exformation by way of longer-term exposure with you directly or indirectly via others you have cultivated relationships with over time. What's more likely when you deal with people different from you is that there are fewer points where your message and information exchanged have connecting points, and thus there is less depth when you communicate. Expanding the width of common exformation increases points of contact with the information resulting in clearer communication.

More exformation leads to greater depth. So, while a message can come with a vast amount of exformation, if that context is not shared (implicitly or

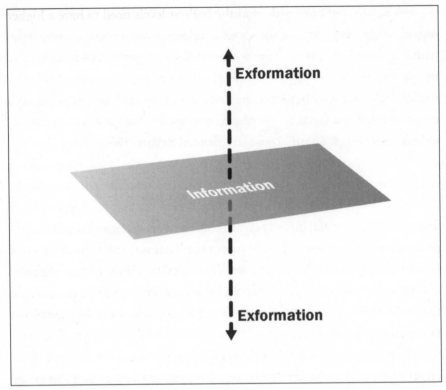

Figure 4

explicitly) so that it connects like a puzzle piece or the "right" Lego™ brick to complete a model, it is likely not very effective.

Recognizing disparate exformation is not easy. "The transfer of exformation takes attentiveness," says Nørretranders. In an organization, the responsibility rests on everyone. Organizations have short attention spans. The need for consistent information and its supporting technology is unquestionable in a firm. Depending on size and degree of information technology adoption, there are multiple channels and systems for communication. For those who communicate more and make more decisions, access to internal and external sources is generally made easier, whether it is confidential information or engagement with leading experts in a discipline of interest.

Conversely, decision-makers at the highest levels need to have a higher degree of attentiveness and effort in developing robust "exformation systems." These efforts may be as crucial as IS/IT systems in which we heavily invest. And while they are not as intensive of a financial investment as information technology, significant time and human capital investment are necessary to build the relational, human technologies that foster greater access to individual and subsequently organizational exformation.

Exformation Systems

There is no precedent in creating an exformation system. Empirical evidence as to direct financial value from organizational investment into this human system or human technology doesn't exist. However, knowing the cost of information and its related technological systems, we can conclude that exformation systems are of significant value given the disparate ratio of exformation to information.

We have yet to create exformation systems intentionally or explicitly in organizations. If we aspired to do so, we would at the least need to create some semblance of guidance or nudges toward their design.

In their book, *Resourceful Exformation*, authors Francis Laleman and George Supreeth write: "Exformation is the process of making things unknown. Exformation flows hither and thither, deconstructing what we already know and opening up a space and a plane and a volume and a time and a word, to be continuously reconstructed and replenished with new meaning—creating new spaces."[21]

Thus, exformation and exformation systems are a product of us being human. We are constantly discarding information and are always making meaning when we do. Any design of an exformation system must have humans or humanity at its center. Exformation system design, like Inclusion Systems development, is for the benefit and development of all stakeholders, internal and external to an organization.

Second, exformation systems are living and generative. Our perhaps most meaningful learning is via our exformation. Learning is central to generative organizational cultures.

Third, exformation systems are open. Everyone owns exformation. It's like when you dive deep into the KonMari Method and start decluttering your home. What do you do with all the stuff you no longer consider necessary for what sparks joy? You put it out on the curb for others who pass by to gain joy from, right? Of course, there are flea markets that allow you to share joy with your neighbors in a moderate exchange of coin and community. Exformation is the same, minus the coin. Flea markets, while sometimes garnering the temporary local vendors financial value, generally are all about the exchange of story, positive energy, and camaraderie.

It's rare that organizations make sense of exclusion's complexity, including the role of exformation. A leader in reflection might think of it like this:

> Our commitment to DEI is about our cultural evolution. At the center of our evolution is creating the space to learn and connect across our various contexts. With such variety, it is likely that there will be times that we are blinded by its complexity. This is natural and human. Being attentive to context prevents our humanness resulting in dehumanizing others. Ostracism is inhumane. It is unacceptable in any form and if you feel like it is happening to you or a colleague, I want to know even if you are not sure if it is what you are experiencing.
>
> The more we can be in dialogue, exploring our diverse exformation, which exists in the hearts of each one of us, the greater our curiosity about and inquiry into who we are, the more we grow individually and collectively, the better off our business is, and the more innovative we become. When we are vigilant in recognition of and consistent in taking actions to appropriately address instances of occlusion and ostracism—and mindful that we are doing all we can to understand context—our collective rivers flow.
>
> —Sincerely, Your CEO

Conversely, I also know that exclusion might be in our failure to take the time to make sense of our common exformation. I was moved by a quote from Francis Laleman: "Training is a vessel being filled. Learning is a river flowing by. Filling a vessel is information, in a permanent illusion of the certainty of a moment. Enabling a river to flow is exformation, embracing the uncertainties of adaptation, evolution and growth."

Mitigating the negative impacts of exclusion is mostly about creating the mechanisms for people to be at least as relational in their work as they are transactional. Leaning heavily into relational ways of being in organizational life is crucial to creating an Inclusion System. Doing so is a critical element in the way forward toward consistently mitigating the harmful impacts of exclusion in all its forms.

Inclusively Aligned
Organizational Design

"When you are solving a problem, you are taking action to have something go away: the problem. When you are creating, you are taking action to have something come into being: the creation. Notice that the intentions of these actions are opposite."

—**Robert Fritz,** *The Path of Least Resistance*

undamental element number one in developing an Inclusion System is that inclusion should be accessible, actionable, and sustainable. For inclusion to be actionable, it must be unambiguously prioritized. When an organization prioritizes something, it does all it can to signal and communicate, build capability, and ultimately deliver on that priority. With such prioritization naturally comes accountability and appropriate resources to meet the expectations that have been created around the priority.

DEI, if prioritized, should naturally get the same treatment. Unfortunately, this is rarely the case. Among the requirements outlined in chapter six, I hold organizational design as one of the most important requirements needed to unambiguously prioritize inclusion *and* align it with purpose.

This chapter will make clear what organizational design is, why it's critical in developing an Inclusion System, as well as provide insights about and examples demonstrating how to think about your organizational design efforts with an inclusive lens.

Organizational Design—The Basics

Organizational design addresses systems, structures, and behaviors, including how decisions are made. Organizational design determines most of what and how people do what they do each day within their organizations. Companies are constantly in the process of doing organizational design. Whether they are doing so in a formal, uniformed manner or not, the design of the organization is in motion. That is, organizations of all sizes form a *strategy*, create *structure* intentionally or consequentially, and create *information systems* and explicit or implicit *ways of working*; they reward and motivate people with pay or other *rewards*; and they *bring people into the organization* and develop them as needed to fill various roles that come with relational and transactional expectations.

If you want to create organizational equity, then the *practice* of inclusion must be a prime variable in the equation to do so. If the design of an organization is made without harvesting the ideas and interests of those impacted by such decisions, then the development of an Inclusion System or anything resembling it will be out of reach.

Inclusively aligned organizational design communicates to employees that their interests—the conditions that need to be created for people to thrive and fulfill the organizational mission—are willingly taken into consideration. One way I define inclusion is an individual's willingness to be influenced by the so-called "other." These others are not alien to the organization. In fact, it is more often that they are organizational influencers who have a different kind of power. They make impact through others. In doing so, they become trusted advisors, mentors, and information sources. They emerge as key nodes in many people's networks, even though the organization may not know how much value their contribution brings to overall strategy fulfillment. Avoiding this hidden mistake is relatively easy. First, be deliberate in the design of your organization. Second, create space so that people can engage with you in the design. Create opportunities for sharing ideas and time to make sense of the ideas shared. Lastly, because organizational design is an iterative process, keep inviting people to the table regularly as the organization evolves and the design adapts to constantly changing needs.

There are a variety of organizational design approaches a firm can choose from. I have adopted the Star Model™ created by organizational design pioneer Dr. Jay Galbraith. Galbraith states, "For an organization to be effective, all the policies must be aligned and interacting harmoniously with one another. Alignment of all policies will communicate a clear, consistent message to the company's employees." The Star Model™ framework consists of five "design policies." Design policies are the components or tools that management, and I argue an entire organization, should become skilled in to make optimal decisions and drive the behavior of the organization.[1]

Figure 5: The Star Model™

The five policies (categories) of the Star Model™ are: *strategy*, which is the company's direction; *structure*, which is about power and influence; *processes*, which reflects how information is shared; *rewards*, which influences motivation; and *people*, which are the skill sets and mindsets needed and expected of all contributors to the organizational mission.

As these components are interdependent and integral to one another, separating them is counterproductive and pragmatically impossible. Nonetheless, this regularly happens. Imagine if the organizational design process itself was perpetually informed by elements of inclusion. What might be possible?

Start with Strategy

Strategy contains the company's vision and values and its formula for success.

The strategy outlines what the company is doing (for and with whom) and, of critical importance to an Inclusion System, how the above will be done. Most essentially, what the strategy component of organizational design does is create clarity of direction, conveying those inclusive ways of being that are non-negotiable.

All organizations want their people to base their decisions and direction on the organizational strategy. And all firms want those actions to translate into sustainable results. These are reasonable expectations. However, clarity of understanding isn't a given around organizational strategy, even for senior personnel. In fact, one study concluded that only 7 percent of employees are clear about their company's strategy and their role and executing it.[2] They continue by stating that the highest performing organizations, those that are "strategy-focused," have an employee base where every employee "understands the strategy and is expected to find improved ways to conduct their day-to-day business so they contribute to the success of that strategy."

I remember interviewing for a newly created diversity and inclusion role at the Novartis Institutes for BioMedical Research (NIBR). My sentiment when invited to come for a series of face-to-face interviews was that it would be fun to visit Cambridge and Boston. I had a couple of consulting prospects

I wanted to meet in person. A few of my friends lived there, and one of my favorite jazz clubs in the US, Wally's Café, is based there. I concluded that while I was tepid on the role, it could be a nice twenty-four to thirty-six hours to do a little business and have a bit of adventure.

Of course, I ended up accepting the job and moving to Cambridge a few months later after twenty years of living in Atlanta. Now, why I took the role had a lot to do with what struck me and stuck with me the whole flight home and week or so prior to letting them know I would accept the offer. That day, the division's founding president, Dr. Mark Fishman, did a presentation where he talked about what he framed as a "Sociology of Innovation." He pretty much got me at the title slide. Simply hearing a world-renowned physician researcher frame his talk around creating a culture of self-organization, entrepreneurial spirit, and collegiality quickly elevated my interest. What preceded him going into detail about creating such a culture is what stayed with me the most. He shared the most elegant summation of an organizational strategy I had ever seen (Figure 6). When unmet need was high and the scientific depth regarding the disease mechanism was high, these were the projects that would be prioritized. I was inspired, and I could tell I was not alone.

What I took away from NIBR in day zero was that everyone had access to the strategy at a high level, allowing them to inquire and be deliberate about how they made sense of what to prioritize, independent of their level of seniority or span of control.

Starting with strategy in an organization's inclusively aligned design does many things. First, it enables ease of prioritization. When all employees are clear about the strategy, they can think holistically about how their strategies at a departmental or systemic level connect to the overall organizational raison d'être. Second, leading with strategy creates a different level of ownership. In most organizations, the strategy won't be crafted by everyone. However, if everyone has access to the strategy and can engage with it in real time as it emerges, evolves, and changes, employees are more likely to make decisions reflective of its intent. Without a clear line of sight,

Research Strategy

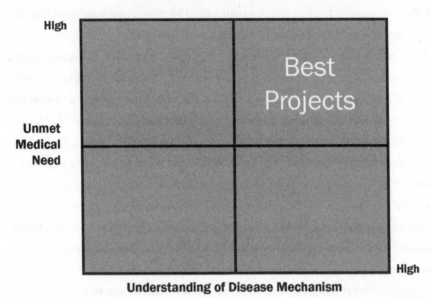

Figure 6

the strategy becomes a black box, and employees' ability to execute on it is at best ambiguous and often occurs as disconnected. The disconnection can happen at all levels and in any area of an organization. It happens a great deal with DEI.

In most of the organizations I've engaged with, inclusion has not been a part of their organizational designs. It has not been aligned with their strategies such that the organization in total knows its value and how it can guide organizational objectives. In large part, DEI has been treated as a favorable but ultimately non-essential feature, kind of like free coffee.[3] This doesn't mean that organizations don't value DEI; it is more so that the act of strategy development in many organizations is exclusive. When a privileged few have exclusive access to the organizational "why," disparity is created that adversely impacts the less privileged majority and the organizational at-large.

People commit to what they help create. Organizations should ask questions such as, "To what extent are leaders, employees, and stakeholders clear on the strategy?" or "How is DEI considered in the development and implementation of strategy?" Questions that create space for all contributors to take ownership in the organizational direction. And while organizations are not democracies, the value of a process that allows for stakeholders who are implementing the strategy to be included from its inception can lead not only to quicker alignment but also to rapid adaptation to inevitable change as it arises.

I believe that many executives consider themselves champions or, at a minimum, supporters of inclusion. Nonetheless, leaders must unambiguously build inclusion principles into organizational strategy. Doing so moves firms away from reactive, representation-focused approaches to reputation management and toward developing organizations where inclusion lives in the values as reflected by expectations and behaviors.

Strategy in organizational design includes values. Just as programmers' values are built into the code they write for an artificial intelligence algorithm, values are reflected in the choices made by the individuals contributing to the creation of an organizational strategy. Thus, whether done explicitly or implicitly, values and strategy go hand in hand. And because values are also a reflection of organizational purpose, strategy mirrors purpose.

One of my clients recognized this and decided to go deep on values. Our original engagement was to work with this medical communications company to create an Inclusion System. During our analysis and assessment phase, the organization was in the process of expansion via two acquisitions. Acquisitions weren't new to the organization. They had fueled impressive and complementary growth for many years of the firm's existence. What was different this time is that it had a new CEO who wanted to grow the company with greater emphasis on core values like togetherness, integrity, caring, trust, team spirit, and innovation. While inclusion wasn't explicitly stated, the implicit nature of inclusion was clear.

Given my client's desire to emphasize values, the Chief People Officer wanted to work with as many people as possible to develop them. Her intention was to co-create the values *with* the organization. So, we invited the entire company to participate in a series of cultural values summits. These summits were held across four continents, open to all employees, and resulted in more than 70 percent of the organization engaging. While the impacts are still manifesting, the short-term benefits have been that people are energized by their participation. They feel included and more connected across the various newly acquired and legacy business areas. Perhaps most importantly, they feel like their voices, perspectives, and presence matters. Through this process, the organization has signaled that inclusion is aligned with purpose. It is inconsequential that the word "inclusion" didn't surface as a final written value because inclusion is in action leading the development of the strategy and organizational design in its totality.

What my client did without it being the original intention was invite the organization's members to participate in the design of the organization, starting with strategy.

Structure Creates Behavior

Water follows the path of least resistance. Have you ever had mold grow in your home? I have. The water didn't insist; it settled and waited, and at some point, with little effort, flowed into whatever miniscule crevice it had access to. Humans are the same. We don't change when we go to work. Organizations indeed follow the path of least resistance in aggregate.

My dad used to share a quote attributed to many, including Benjamin Franklin: "A [hu]man convinced against [its] will is of the same opinion still."

Dr. Mona Sue Weissmark and others have advised that making people feel like they are wrong is not a recipe for greater inclusion.[4] Yet, many in the DEI space are committing increased resources to conversations about privilege and concepts such as "white fragility." It is worthwhile to engage in these levels of dialogue. However, the purpose should be non-linear learning. Otherwise, many people will opt out of such conversations, even if these conversations are popular and their proponents want to make the world a more humanistic place.

Trying to change behaviors now is the goal of many who desire to facilitate change with a focus on a particular in-group or cause. The strategy is to change a group different than theirs—one that has historically had more power—and to do so by giving information that says to those deemed to be the perpetrators (usually, but not limited to, white blokes) of harmful behaviors that they are bad and that they need to start doing things differently. Whether it is because of unconscious preferences or not, the so-called perpetrators are implicitly those in the wrong who need to change, and a selected group (like DEI practitioners) is there to tell them how.

Robert Fritz says, "People commonly believe that if they change their behavior, they can change the structures in their lives. In fact, just the opposite is true." Fritz also notes, "Structure determines behavior. The way anything is structured determines the behavior within that structure."[5] What this means is that the blaming, shaming, and naming will be absolutely meaningless (and potentially negatively reinforcing undesired outcomes) if it is not targeting the structure.

In the Star Model™, structure and power go hand in hand. Decision-making authority as connected to the strategy drives resources and increases agency in those offices and roles the organizational leadership believes will be most instrumental in achieving its short-term goals. Power is mostly awarded circumstantially and by the nature of a growing enterprise's changes. This means that there are times when some departments are depended upon more than others.

For example, for the past seven or eight years, the budget for digital business across most enterprises has increased dramatically, and some companies have created roles like Chief Digital Officer (CDO, not to be confused with Chief Diversity Officer, which has a similar acronym).[6] This role has often been given a great deal of resources and agency. They usually report to the CEO and are involved in or leading all the initiatives that will move the company through its "digital transformation." A role like this, by nature, must be inclusive. Most CDOs are dealing with everything from R&D to existing products and the roll out, acquisition, and co-licensing of new products. Many times, they have other powerful roles reporting to them (e.g., Chief Information Officer [CIO] and/or Chief Technology Officer). With the power that is designed into their offices, the way the office runs could be a prime example of inclusion in action.

Now, the CDO office is not the only one that can do that simply because of the nature of the role. In fact, it's possible that all offices, budget prioritized or not, can make more informed, insightful, and impactful contributions to the organization when the organization is inclusively designed to intersect with all its component parts. This is not to say that everyone just runs around speaking to one another without purpose. What it means is that the organizational structure is designed to maximize the open flow of information, access, and opportunity to influence decisions. Power's role is one of helping create more space for sharing ideas and information. It should not be about amassing more influence or dictating organizational rules of engagement.

Power always exists inside of an organizational structure. However, it changes based on priorities, position, role purpose, and project. That means structure in the design of the organization should take power into account, not only based on the boxes of its organogram, but also on how such power might be utilized and the purpose it serves. As Professor Sukhvinder Obhi, a leading neuroscience researcher who studies power, states, "If leaders are not educated and coached around power, they may unwittingly undermine the journey toward better outcomes in diverse groups. The goal should be to understand power and educate leaders (at all levels) in how to use power for fostering inclusion, distinctiveness and psychological safety needs (and associated improvements in work quality)."

Obhi continues in conveying that, given the influence of power holders in the management of change, any consideration of inclusion as it relates to shifting sociocultural norms and transforming mindsets or behaviors, on an individual or collective level, without the consideration of power (and, in this case, as it relates to organization structure), is incomplete, at best.

As a consultant and an employee, I have been in a variety of situations where structure was inclusively designed and thus aligned, and in other situations where it was not. The typical process of designing a new departmental structure is that a few people, usually those with the most bureaucratic and hierarchical power, determine that a new way forward is needed. Of course, it is hoped that they are responding to what the organization needs, but they haven't necessarily consulted with those who will be impacted most by the decisions made. It is not always clear that the decisions are based on what delivers the best overall outcomes for all the interdependent stakeholders who will be affected by their design choices.

In one company I was a part of, inclusion was not considered. A major decision about reporting lines and the governance of the DEI function was made in private. Some people who were needed to help with the operational changes were informed of the decision. Others who were most impacted by the decision, like me, were left sensing that something was in the process of change but not getting any clear communication. Then, when the change was set in motion, I was informed right before everyone else would be made aware. The abrupt nature of this type of change is confusing and can occur as the peak of an ostracizing experience. The reality is that it is unnecessary and creates the opposite effect of what an inclusive leader would be interested in facilitating. What would have been different if I had been informed about the upcoming changes?

I may have been equally unhappy with it. That is organizational life. And, if the communication would have been transparent, giving me time to make sense of it, I would have been able to get onboard with the decision, rather than spend months doing so after I had discovered it from a third party. My matrixed managers only informed me after I asked (with the new third-party information in hand) for the fifth time.

This story illustrates how not to create structure and use power in an inclusive organizational design. I have also been a part of redesigns where those impacted were informed as the process started. In the case of a hospital client, they started with a question like this one: "Do the structures and ways of working facilitate inclusion, collaboration, partnerships, and shared learning?" This is a question one would ask when committed to inclusively aligned organizational design.

By putting a version of this question forward to all stakeholders who would be impacted by the changes, they were able to conclude that certain structural changes would be necessary to meet the emerging expectations of their colleagues and for their customers (patients and their families). This meant that some people who were reporting to the head of a group would have to report one manager removed. And while there were some initial concerns about access to the group head, they agreed that a change in managers didn't mean a change in communication. Their default was that, when in doubt of who to go to, share broadly. Keep direct line managers involved but engage with whomever was deemed best equipped to respond to an inquiry. Over time, the group was able to become clearer on whom to contact and collaborate with for what, experientially creating greater efficiency.

Even though much of the time spent considering power in organizations is focused on structure, there is not often a detailed and explicit exploration of power. In fact, many who practice components of organizational design attempt to make their organizations flatter with the intention of de-emphasizing hierarchy. The belief of these organizations is that exchanging a more hierarchical structure for a matrixed one enables greater collaboration. The intention is for a leader or group of leaders working together to create a department where various functions operate in a complementary, interdependent manner.

Sometimes this works, as in the hospital department example above. In its case, the leaders exerted power in a way that is conducive to fostering business and people outcomes intended to be helpful to everyone. In other cases, working to create a flatter organization or any organizational structure fails because in trying to distribute power to mitigate information bottlenecks, there is no explicit expectation on how leaders should use their power.

All organizations, whether through their organizational design process or otherwise as part of their learning, should be clear about power and how to use it to help people thrive. Six types of managerial power are often talked about in the literature: 1) legitimate (formal or bureaucratic power); 2) reward power; 3) coercive power (power by force); 4) expert power; 5) referent power; and 6) reciprocal power. All six of these will be at play in your organization. Two of them, expert and referent power, are likely to provide an environment (particularly among knowledge workers) that has greater capacity for adaptation and working through the increasing and inevitable complexity of organizations. The sixth, reciprocal power, is a substance that one should focus on for its Inclusion System.

If you have worked in organizations for any period, you have likely experienced all six types of power. I don't hold that certain types of power are generally better than others. For example, in some cases, legitimate power or formal power is necessary. When dealing with situations in organizations or geographies where the formal rules and regulations are not adhered to, potentially putting the organization or its people in harm's way, articulating what an individual or external stakeholder can lose is an appropriate and often effective course of action. However, in most contemporary circumstances, creating an atmosphere that leads to concern or fear about one's financial well-being, reputation, and status may appear as immediately effective, but it rarely produces the kind of effort that creates sustainable company growth. In fact, a lot of time can be spent in resistance to this use of power in legal, psychological, diplomatic, and directly confrontational ways.

Conversely, the three types of power that are more appropriate for modern organizations and are instrumental in the construction of an inclusion system are: expert, referent, and reciprocal power. *Expert power* is when a manager is given influence over a team based on their superior knowledge, insights, and expertise alongside a proven track record of performance. Expert power is preferred when designing an organization for inclusion as it has the potential to level the playing field. Tap into expert power for designing inclusive systems. There is a certain egalitarian feel to expert power that lends to broader inclusion in decision-making. Expert power has a dark side, though. If experts become dictatorial and exhibit control rather than enable learning and foster better solutions, they de-energize and derail the development of a system of inclusion.

If organizational design is done inclusively and expert power is preferred and rewarded, the design must have corresponding rewards for a key behavior that makes expert power worth having—information sharing. Information sharing is crucial for *reward* power. When it is done robustly and amply rewarded, expert power may be among the best uses of power in organizational life. Why? Because when the best ideas win, everyone wins.

However, making this practice consistent requires aligned team/group goals. The goals must be interdependent. Interdependence is a critical element in inclusively aligned organizational design and it is a foundational element in the development of an Inclusion System. I have mentioned interdependence a lot. It is critical for Inclusion Systems. And it is not a panacea. Some societal cultures that value interdependence may also value sameness.[7] Be mindful of the influence of how cultural values can negatively influence ways of being that are predominantly positive.

Self-preservation and the fear of loss makes broadly sharing information too risky for some and, in the case of some organizations, prohibited. Whether it is to external potential collaborators, peers, or superiors, the incentives for sharing must be clear and the perceived benefits unambiguously articulated.

Referent power is a valuable tool in the power spectrum. It is the power that comes from being respected and having credibility. Leaders with referent power have a known history of building trust through actions and results. Since trust is a critical element in making inclusion normative in any organization, referent power is a must. Conversely, there are some people who will try to associate themselves with a leader for personal gain or take on the behaviors of a leader to feel part of the in-group. Thus, while referent power is needed to create an inclusive culture, its shadow side, groupthink, must be monitored for.

In one organization I worked with in the management consulting industry, I recall observing a meeting where a managing partner was prone to being more inquisitive than advocating (regularly sharing perspectives throughout the meeting). His tendency was to listen, listen some more, watch the responses of the people in the room, and then listen some more. Then, after the discussion had gained momentum, he would ask a question that spoke to the issue, addressed and surfaced underlying tensions and conflicts, and required the majority of the people in the room to contribute to assure that it could be answered sufficiently. He had been at the company for twenty years, and many of those at director level and above had been in the company with him for at least ten years. Some of them mirrored his style consciously or unconsciously at least in part because it worked. They did so even if it wasn't their natural style. Of course, as an external who preferred this way of leading, I thought it was great and that everyone should be like the people who hired me to come in and work with the firm.

I was at best incomplete in my consideration. While this leader's incisive style was preferred by many, it was newer to some directors and partners who hadn't worked with or for him for long. To them, it seemed as if he was looking to make them look stupid by not engaging in the conversation earlier on and sharing his thoughts. Who was right? There wasn't a right or wrong way to engage. What was necessary was that everyone needed to be familiar with and respect the styles of all contributors at the table and recognize the benefit when one style predominates or equally informs discussions. If the exchanges of a decision-making meeting that includes a respected manager's imprint on a junior organizational member in a positive way can lead that person to match the values and behaviors that align with the intentions and strategy of the organization, referent power can be quite beneficiary. Style is much less important than sustainable function.

While referent power creates norms via the mirroring of leaders' virtues, *reciprocal power* is about making intentional contributions to others for their growth and development toward meeting organizational objectives. Reciprocal power is what Ed Schein calls "helping." Helping is as complex and variable as businesses and their members are. What Schein makes clear is that "help is the action of one person that enables another person to solve a problem, to accomplish something, or to make something easier."[8] Reciprocal power is all about finding ways to contribute authentically and meaningfully to the so-called other, to help them thrive and contribute their best.

In summary, power is an inevitable element of organizations. Different types of power enable different types of structures. While all six types of power are generally prevalent in any organization of a moderate size, organizations that consider expert, referent, and reciprocal power as preferred modes of the expression of power have likely designed their organization inclusively. Of course, while structures are reflective of power and its expression, they aren't exclusively so.

Processes and Rewards

In his book *The Path of Least Resistance*, author Robert Fritz shares an interesting story about the city of Boston. "The Boston roads were actually formed by utilizing existing cow paths," he writes. "But how did these cow paths come to be? The cow moving through the topography tended to move where it was immediately easiest to move . . . Each time cows passed through the same area, it became easier for them to take the same path they had taken the last time, because the path became more and more clearly defined. Thus, the structure of the land gave rise to the cows' consistent pattern of behavior in moving from place to place. As a result, city planning in Boston gravitates around the mentality of the seventeenth-century cow."[9]

Fritz's example speaks to the structure of the landscape influencing the flow of the cows, and we can equate this to organizational structure creating the flow of information through *processes*. The Star Model™ deals with informal, business, and managerial processes.

Informal processes can be described as voluntary. People self-organize to develop mechanisms to share information, meet short- and longer-term needs for groups with similar interests, and move toward strategy execution. These multiple exchanges serve the needs of the people who are deployed on specific tasks at particular times and have clear needs to execute on the task. Historically, information would, by nature of the mechanisms to share, remain within a nested group. Now, advanced organizational connectivity allows for these self-organized groups to influence the organization in ways never previously possible. Technologies that have evolved over the past five to ten years, like enterprise and public social networks, communication platforms, messaging apps, wikis, blogs, and intranet pages, allow for intergroup and organization-wide sharing. In the process of inclusive organizational design, these exchanges are data that inform the process. As design is not a discrete event, the information produced by these informal networks are part of the energy source that powers its refinement. Over time, if the organizational design is indeed created in an inclusive manner, the feedback, insights, and solicited inputs from these networks inform the future, foster agility, and increase the potential for everyone to thrive and contribute their best to the mission.

Once you have had a good mentor, you are very clear about the impact they can have on your life and career. You can give a testimony about the power they have to broaden your mind, network, and nudge you to grow in ways that you may not have previously imagined. I saw the magic of mentoring evolve while working at the research division of Novartis. Learning about informal structures led me to see mentoring as an input that every organization developing an Inclusion System should implement.

While it is not straightforward to measure the impact of these programs, I can confirm that a large percentage of the mentor community have received internal promotions at all levels in the organization, have been recruited for bigger roles outside of the organization (often lauded for their commitment to mentoring), and are leading key projects with aplomb. Mentoring served as a catalyst for individual and organizational growth.

The momentum for that mentoring came from self-organizing and was subsequently further informed by the DEI office taking the opportunity to measure the networks of the organization that reflected the culture of mentoring we were seeing unfold. This example is one of many that speaks to the need for organizational design to be inclusively informed and to generatively evolve via listening and engagement across emerging self-organized processes.

As a part of *process* within the Star Model™, there are also both business and managerial processes. Business processes should be monitored, and there should be active efforts to refine these processes to reduce redundancy, increase efficiency, and lower cost. The business processes should be equally about freeing up people resources so that those driving the managerial processes can spend their limited time engaged in listening to teams, customers, and partners to refine management processes in a more inclusive manner.

Often, managers get caught up focusing on automation for the purpose of eliminating anything that seems like it is overusing resources. This line of thinking is not unfounded. Currently, a predominant global narrative is that jobs will be lost because of automated business processes. This is without dispute.[10] However, what can also be deduced is that human and managerial processes will require an even greater capacity to operate with business systems in a manner that continuously optimizes both rather than seeks to displace one for the other. Business systems cannot practice inclusion, at least not in a way that is reflective of the relational construct framed in this text. Managerial systems, which are generally operating around more complexity, can. In fact, for all systems to be optimized, inclusive practice is necessary. The nature of the Star Model™, with all of its interdependencies and the fact that everything flows from strategy through structure and into process, rewards, and people, necessitates such.

Rewards are generally straightforward. In the Star Model™, they consist of compensation practices, promotions, job challenges, and recognition systems (i.e., stories about their achievements in company communications, on-the-spot awards of cash, high-end gifts, hotel/vacations, and other monetary equivalents). While compensation is generally at the top of the list when it comes to the most desired motivation for people in an organization, it is often easy to duplicate elsewhere and is inherently individual. In many cases, there are rarely factors in compensation that speak to inclusion.

Most reward systems are not designed for inclusion. They build in competition between team members and may encourage behavior contrary to the values promoted as core to an inclusive corporate culture. Conversely, if rewards are designed in tandem with the influence and intentions of an Inclusion System, they are more likely to reflect the principles of inclusion and meet people and enterprise needs. It's not always easy to know if your rewards reflect inclusion. You can start to diagnose this by asking, "Is inclusion and equity built into metrics and scorecards to discover benefits for all stakeholders? Are mechanisms and forums in place to incorporate people's input and inform the organization about the prevalence of inclusive behaviors?"

Organizations can give many types of rewards, and those rewards generally follow a path of reinforcing certain outcomes either with or without considering how they are achieved. The highest likelihood is that the rewards will reflect *what* was achieved, not *how* they were. This means that the behavior of those rewarded will also mirror what the structure has created as its least resistant path. When rewards are shaped and informed by a system of inclusion, the rewards will be reflective of those behaviors. They won't simply be based on the conveniences of the past that are mostly based on monetary returns alone. Thinking about inclusion being sustained means that your organization considers the long-term "how" things get done at least as much as it considers the "what."

For example, in a high-performance organization where the commercial sales targets are X, the expectation at a minimum would be generating revenue equal to X. In a typical organization, a fictional sales leader (who we will name Petra) who exceeds sales target X year over year would be amply rewarded for such performance. In a system where rewards or people components of an organizational design are constructed without inclusion in mind, it doesn't matter *how* those numbers are achieved. The ends justify the means. The way Petra acts toward their team, partners, collaborators, colleagues, or customers matters much less than those results.

In an organizational design informed by inclusion, the *how* is paramount. This means that if another sales leader (we will call them Ty) just barely meets sales target X year over year but engages the greater ecosystem in a manner that enables other stakeholders to thrive, it's considered worthy of reward at least equal to that which Petra received in exceeding their target. If the organization is very much invested in its inclusion system, it is possible that the rewards for Ty are greater than those for Petra; Ty was invested not just in their primary responsibility, but also in contributing to the elevation of the organization at large. This is rare, but when people processes, particularly mindsets oriented toward inclusion, intersect with reward systems that confirm and reinforce the value of this behavior, it is much easier to see the value of an inclusion orientation.

Further, the net result of the actions of Ty can likely be traced to less negative impacts on people growth—and by extension business outcomes. Ty understands this either through experience, intuition, senior leadership role models, and/or formal training and education. Petra, on the other hand, feels justified as the organizational design of rewards and people is based on hitting targets, and consideration of anything beyond that is deemed to be out of scope or irrelevant in their experience. Petra believes that their job is to meet targets; Ty believes that meeting target goals is only part of their job, while the most important job is to contribute to the growth of the enterprise. Petra operates like most people in organizations do. This is not wrong per se. However, in an inclusively designed organization committed to fostering an organizational mindset of inclusion, all managers are asked to think about how to elevate the entirety of the firm, while simultaneously meeting individual objectives. Ty operates like this, and if their organization is committed to rewarding and reinforcing these values in other ways, inclusive ways of being are sustainable. Naturally, inclusion is further embedded into the organizational mind, as well.

Through the example of sales leaders Petra and Ty, we can see how interdependent organizational design policies are. In the case of the policy *people*, all other parts of the organizational design (i.e., strategy, structure, processes, and rewards) influence how every employee in an organization absorbs and reflects the expectations the combined policies have created.

Early in my DEI career, I was profoundly impacted by a conversation I had with two people I consider among the most strategically minded practitioners in the space, Steve Pemberton (previously an executive leader at Monster.com and Walgreens, currently CHRO at Workhuman) and Tyronne Stoudemire (previously leading DEI at Aon Hewitt and Mercer, and currently VP and Global Chief Diversity and Internal Officer of the Hyatt Corporation). We were standing room only outside of a conference plenary, and I joined their conversation where they were talking about all things people. I was a sponge as these two waxed philosophically and practically about people strategy.

One thing Steve said in response to Tyronne talking about diversity and inclusion in hiring and growing talent stood out to me (I paraphrase): "Development begins during the recruitment process." I have carried that idea with me ever since that day. In fact, when I think about designing people practices in an organizational design today, it deeply informs my thinking around the entirety of the candidate/employee experience. When I think about what it will take for each team member to thrive in an organization, it includes everything from the first communication with the company all the way through the time they exit the firm.

Organizations designed with inclusion in mind consider all elements of the Star Model™ when formally or informally engaged in organizational design. Strategy, of course, is the genesis of any organizational design. An organization's mission, vision, and values cascade and intersect with who is determined to require certain resources and positional authority, how things are done, incentives, and the mindsets of leaders and followers. If strategy is created in a vacuum, then the probability of the organizational design going beyond such an approach is low. Any system, even one like human anatomy and physiology, develops based on its inputs and outputs. If nutrition and lifestyle choices are not strengthening the organism, the inevitable result is decline. Organizations are the same. If there is a belief (even a theoretical one) that inclusion is vital to organizational evolution, then organizations must determine what inclusion is and then design for it to be deliberately and unambiguously prioritized.

What does it mean for an organizational leader to utilize organizational design in order to unambiguously prioritize inclusion?

> We are committed to creating a culture of inclusion—inclusion as a normative way of being. What this means is that as our strategy is developed, and more so as it emerges, it is critical that it will drive all aspects in the design of our organization. All parts of the Star Model™, or any other organizational design approach, can affect employee behavior and influence performance and culture. They work in concert, interdependently. We absolutely expect high levels of performance along with a robust culture. And we believe that an inclusively aligned organizational design creates greater possibilities for all aspects of organizational life to evolve. That implies that everyone is meaningfully included in designing our organization and continuously making sense of what is needed to generate dynamic impact and inspire the extraordinary.
>
> —Sincerely, Your CEO

Cultural Intelligence

"Every human is like all other humans, some other humans, and
no other human."

—**Clyde Kluckhohn**

S everal years ago, I was leading an enterprise-wide project related to
creating inclusive cultures that included a major workstream on flexibility. Before the advent of COVID-19, many organizations were
discussing flexibility related to remote working. The lens for DEI among
most firms was related to long commutes, productivity, and parenting. The
value in working from home for those experiencing long commutes, logis-
tical complexity for caregivers, or some sort of physical or mental disablement requiring accommodation was relatively easy to see for both those who
desired it and those who had to approve it. Conversely, if someone wanted
to work from home because they preferred it or because it better fit their
lifestyle, it occurred differently for many. The point here is not the work-
from-home situation; it's what transpired as we were moving the related
projects forward.

While I was the "owner" of the bigger workstream, I was not directly in charge of leading the flexibility work. When the project was reported on during meetings, it seemed to me like the overall framing was incomplete and lacking momentum. I knew there were conversations going on in the background with a variety of senior leaders who were based in corporate headquarters, but they were shrouded in secrecy and only revealed to a privileged few. Even as the overall project team leader for the work, I was not transparently informed about the bigger picture. It was perplexing. Not only because I was the team leader, but also because I had been doing a significant body of work in a smaller part of the organization exploring remote working—organizational sentiments, barriers, and possibilities to changing policy. From my perspective, I was more experienced, in charge of the overall body of work, and was forthright in offering my time and that of the larger team to help accelerate the efforts.

It didn't matter how much I offered. My commitment to any needed assistance was inconsequential. My colleague didn't recognize that my motivations were solely toward making progress and producing the greatest impact for our colleagues around the world. Nor were they aware that my context had nothing to do with proximity to power. They were more oriented toward status, and organizational hierarchy mattered greatly to them. Conversely, my status orientation is relatively low. Their orientation was to plan with heavy detail, leaving no stone unturned. That is, they wanted to figure out and anticipate most of what we would do first, next, and perhaps never, while I lean toward experimenting, prototyping, and improving along the way. They thought I was questioning their competence and credibility.

Both parties were frustrated, and at least part of it had to do with me not leaning into my cultural intelligence (CQ). The implications damaged the relationship and left the overall body of work compromised. While I was disappointed by the outcome, the learning was invaluable. If I had thought about the way my colleague was responding to me, relationally, with the culturally intelligent lens I thought I had employed on countless occasions, perhaps we could have worked effectively. Then again, maybe not. We may have remained on separate pages. Nonetheless, I wished I had more effectively used my CQ training so that I could have had a before-and-after comparison.

Values matter. Our curiosity and drive in how we engage with difference matters. What we do in cross-cultural interactions with people (which are a lot more frequent than we think) matters. And, of course, as we draw conclusions and make decisions in and for our organization, our capacity to reflect about our thinking matters. Cultural intelligence considers all of the above. Therefore, I consider this requirement an essential skill set for organizations that desire to develop Inclusion Systems.

What Is Cultural Intelligence?

Cultural intelligence is a set of capabilities that allows one to function effectively across cultures. It allows one to be more mindful and reflective about their own culture and others' beliefs that impact their interactions and responses.

There are a few models for cultural intelligence. How it is applied in those models differs. Some applications are intended for marketing purposes and are focused on generating data that assist companies in identifying what is trending using artificial intelligence to harvest unsolicited social data related to things such as sentiment, demographics, and psychographics.

For the most part, those that follow the lines of modern marketing use advanced analytics to dissect and strategize how to maximize market penetration in certain demographic groups. The tools are newer, but the mechanisms are historically similar. Lili Gil Valletta of CIEN+ has expanded their application of cultural intelligence in the creation of the cultural intelligence excellence index (Cix). This tool allows businesses to assess their business cultural intelligence through cross-cultural analytics, metrics, rewards, and senior leader buy-ins with the intention of impacting commercial growth.

The marketing-centric approach expands the reach of cultural intelligence. For some firms, it also potentially reimagines cultural intelligence as a catchall phrase to generate additional information for the purposes of extracting data insights from potential consumers. While the purpose and functioning of the tools from the Gil Valletta group are helpful, the way traditional business co-opts them could be a distraction from the role that CQ plays in the relational construct of inclusion. Organizations can easily move toward the belief that cultural intelligence is optimally used for transactions with others under the pretense that their data are making them more capable of understanding consumer needs.

In answering the question of how to make inclusion more accessible, actionable, and sustainable, CQ provides significant insight. The model of CQ that I will reference is that of Soo Ang and Linn Van Dyne, further expanded by David Livermore. There are several reasons why I prefer this model. In full disclosure, this is what I recommend for my clients. It is what I am certified in and have the most familiarity with.

Based on the concept of general intelligence, "CQ is conceptualized as a specific form of intelligence focused on an individual's ability to grasp and reason correctly in situations characterized by cultural diversity." The domains of CQ reflect notions of applied intelligence, such as emotional intelligence, but are motivated by the reality that diversity and distinctions are inevitable in global organizations and institutions where people interact and are increasingly interdependent.[1]

The construction of cultural intelligence is reflective of "real-world" intelligence and aligns with the contemporary view of intelligence as complex and multidimensional. Ang and Van Dyne repurposed their four dimensions based on human intelligence research and its many cultural contexts.[2] Their conclusion was that intelligence outside of its cultural influences is a [Westernized] mythological construct. Naturally, there are some aspects of intelligence that transcend cultures, particularly the mental processes underlying intelligence and the mental representations upon which they act. Yet, these operations play out differently in terms of what performance looks like from one culture to another. If an individual or an organization assesses performance, then culture and values play a role in how they arrive at their conclusions.

The four factors of CQ are Motivational, Cognitive, Metacognitive, and Behavioral. We will explore these and their importance in building a skill set for actionable inclusion. The Cultural Intelligence Center has named these domains respectively for non-academic consumption as CQ Drive, CQ Knowledge, CQ Strategy, and CQ Action.

CQ Drive: Intrinsic and Extrinsic Motivation for Functioning in Novel Cultural Settings

For many, CQ Drive is one of the highest scoring domains when taking the Cultural Intelligence Center's CQ Self-Assessment. Intrinsically or extrinsically, many individuals are motivated to interact effectively across different cultures. Their motivation may be anything from affinity with a particular culture and wanting a deeper relationship with it to being placed in a new culture (i.e., physical location, organization, team, relationship across differences, etc.) and wanting to be successful in their interactions.

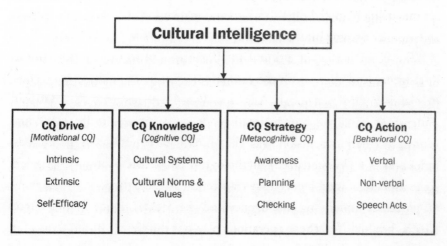

Figure 7[3]

When I was in public health school, I researched violence as a public health issue. I was not only interested in interpersonal violence or intimate assaults; I found the structural dynamics that created the context for higher levels of violence in some locations and among certain communities. These structural elements could be found across the world. One place that came to my attention was a situation in Brazil, particularly among homeless and orphaned children in the slums in Rio de Janeiro, São Paulo, and Salvador, among other large metropolitan areas.

These children—poor, uneducated, desperate, exploited, and mostly Black and Brown—spent their days doing whatever they could to survive and mentally escape from the confines of a nearly inescapable circumstance. My interest in this tragic narrative and how it related to similar dynamics around violence in Black and Brown communities in the United States motivated me to learn more about Brazil, including its language and culture. I eventually traveled there, did some business, research, and most importantly, developed meaningful relationships. Intrinsically, I have always been curious about cultures beyond those I know best. Extrinsically, in my experience with Brazil, I became more familiar with a new culture as a pathway to telling stories and making impact in people's lives on a global scale.

The time I spent in Brazil over three-plus years also served to increase my comfort level when the conversations about moving to Switzerland, my current residence, began. Like many expats around the world, the newness of living outside of your home country is exciting. The motivating factors, like experiencing new people, sights, sounds, and tastes, are easy. What is perhaps more challenging and requires the acquisition of skills is the component of CQ Drive that relates to self-efficacy. While motivation for the cross-cultural engagements might be high when self-reported, the confidence in one's capacity to navigate them transcends willingness alone.

About eighteen months after moving to Switzerland, I took a CQ Self-Assessment + CQ360 (with raters around the world) through the Cultural Intelligence Center. My personal rating of CQ Drive (along with all my scores) had changed, particularly my intrinsic and extrinsic interests.

All have decreased. It is clear to me that my comfort level in communicating with people has diminished. My language skills in High German are at a basic level, and for Swiss German, less so. Thus, when encountering a Swiss neighbor, I mostly listen, smile, and nod yes. They likely know that I am language challenged from when I do utter words in German. I imagine when my German-speaking abilities get better, my overall intrinsic and extrinsic interests of CQ Drive can rise to match my personal (and raters') self-efficacy, which ironically increased in contrast to my interests. I can only hope, but hope will be useless without intentionally building my language skills.

What's important to know about CQ is that it can be constantly improved. In the case of CQ Drive, it can be influenced by CQ Knowledge. CQ Drive, especially self-efficacy (see Figure 7), can contribute to elevating one's CQ Strategy and Action. It is easy to begin thinking that you have "figured out" your cultural intelligence. DEI practitioners are not immune to this phenomenon either.

This mental trap is a bias known as the Dunning-Kruger effect. It is a mind bug that arises due to a lack of self-reflection leading one to think they know more or in some cases may consider themselves an expert in a domain in which they are incompetent (or less so than they think). According to the Cornell University psychologists David Dunning and Justin Kruger, whom this cognitive bias is named after, "Those with limited knowledge in a domain suffer a dual burden: Not only do they reach mistaken conclusions and make regrettable errors, but their incompetence robs them of the ability to realize it."[4]

Disrupting the Dunning-Kruger effect is possible. In fact, metacognition, a skill that enhances CQ when improved, is perhaps a key to overcoming this blind spot. When you step back and think about it, it sounds a bit counterintuitive to think you know as much about a subject that you have minimally explored as you do about one in which you have done advanced study. Of course, it's different when there are adjacent and overlapping connections to a subject area.

Yet, even when there is intersecting knowledge, breadth and depth are not equal, and thinking this way can lead to a variety of problems in organizational life that emerge in team engagement and one-to-one interactions. We will speak more to metacognition when discussing CQ Strategy below. Prior to that, we will explore CQ Knowledge.

CQ Knowledge: Cultivating a Rich Understanding of Culture Norms and Values and How They Affect How People Think and Behave

CQ Knowledge is what I first thought about when I encountered the term "cultural intelligence." After years working in and around the space of cultural competence, particularly in healthcare, I figured that a focus on CQ meant that I needed to have a repertoire of knowledge about a variety of cultures. I needed to know how much to bow with Japanese people, for instance. I figured that it would be helpful for me to recognize that in various part of the world, a grasshopper could be a pet, a pest, or a complete source of protein.

The following image comes from HSBC, which has created ads that have become memes for those of us who work in the space of diversity and cultural

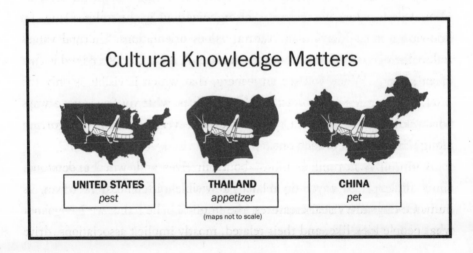

intelligence. Their ads emphasize the need for relevant cultural knowledge. And, while such information is important, to make CQ Knowledge all about knowing particular aspects about localities that you may be spending time or doing business in is grossly incomplete. It is much, much more.

CQ Knowledge is about understanding cultural artifacts, legal and economic structures, family and educational systems, and spiritual and social values, as well as their associated assumptions. It is about context and goes beyond more traditional visible and non-visible diversity dimensions into those things that make us unique both inherently and from that which has been acquired. CQ Knowledge, more than most constructs, lends itself to being oriented to multiple dimensions of diversity as discussed in previous chapters.

Intersectionality is often limited to the theoretical, but CQ Knowledge is an applied, constantly evolving complement for working with multidimensional organizations and people. If you want to refine your ability to recognize subtle distinctions (zoom in) and see complexity in relation to contexts or perspectives (zoom out), especially those related to individuals that make up teams and organizations at large, growing your depth and breadth of cultural knowledge can be a fruitful path forward.

Cultural Values

What stands out as most relevant for organizations in the realm of cultural knowledge is the domain of cultural values orientations. Cultural values reflect the diversity that is under the surface. A metaphor often used is that of an iceberg. When you see an iceberg, that which is visible is only the proverbial tip. When it comes to cultural values, what you see is not always what you get. Cultural values are universal—everyone can be categorized along the spectrum of each one.

Cultural values tell us more about ourselves and, when understood, about others than anything related to visible differences. However, as human beings are visual creatures, the implicit beliefs that we have about what people look like, and their related, mostly implicit associations, drive much of our perception and behavioral interactions. The limits of perception are clear. What is less clear is how limiting the cognitive anchors that we develop due to visual cues and related stereotypes are for organizations with increasingly diverse workforces and talent pools.

What are cultural values? Cultural values are the predominant archetypes of how significant numbers of people from a respective country or region function. These archetypes can be perceived as stereotypical in the negative sense. This perception would be true if we made the fundamental attribution error of assigning limiting descriptions to all people that represent a particular geography or culture. In the case of how we will look at cultural values, these are more like what cross-cultural psychologists Joyce Osland and Allan Bird call "sophisticated stereotypes"—broad relative differences based on empirical data from research on various cultures.

Sophisticated stereotypes are helpful. They allow for people to gain a general understanding of how and why people from different cultures may respond situationally in particular ways. These models present a way of explaining contrasting behaviors across cultures. A conceptual understanding could be extracted by learning about one's own and others' cultural generalities as presented in the table on the following page replicating that of Osland and Bird.[5] The authors recommend that students and employees learn about these common cultural dimensions.

These are critical components of self- and other-awareness in business settings. My experience when first engaging with a cultural values assessment was that my scores in many domains were not consistent with Western, Anglo norms but were more in alignment with the norms of Confucian Asia. I am now more cooperative than competitive, lean toward collectivism instead of individualism, and consider the long-term impact of decisions more than I do the short-term. This was a bit surprising at first. However, once I thought about my influential mentors and friends, many of whom are from Confucian Asia, it made sense. I have, for a considerable amount of time, been willing to be influenced by them.

Common Cultural Dimensions

Being	Containing and controlling	Doing
Human nature as changeable		Human nature as unchangeable
Monochronic time		Polychronic time
High-context language		Low-context language
Low uncertainty avoidance		High uncertainty avoidance
Low power distance		High power distance
Short-term orientation		Long-term orientation
Individualism		Collectivism
Diffuse		Particularism
Inner-directed		Emotional
Individualism (competition)		Specific
Analyzing (reductivist)		Outer-directed
		Group-organization (collusion)
		Synthesizing (larger, integrated wholes)

Sources: Kluckhohn & Strodtbeck (1961); Hall & Hall (1990); Holstede (1980); Parsons & Shils (1951); Trompenaars & Hampden Turner (1993); Trompenaars (1994). The dimensions are bipolar continua, with the first six containing midpoints.

Table 3

My score in and of itself could not explain the context regarding who I spend my time with and am influenced by to others who read my results. Nor would it confirm whether my tendencies via self-reporting would match what I would say, do, or what perceptions I would form in response to others. It would provide a starting point for inquiry, a set of hypotheses.

Osland and Bird highlight that while these binary sophisticated stereotypes are valuable for us to understand, doing so in absence of context is shortsighted. They frame this by presenting examples of how these archetypes (Table 3 above) that many have learned can lead to a person jumping to an incomplete conclusion. That is, they equate the cultural values that correlate with where someone and/or their ancestors originate from geographically as "the way *they* are." This was not the intention of Dutch social psychologist Geert Hofstede and other cross-cultural theorists. In fact, Hofstede was clear that a construct like people from Confucian Asia being oriented toward collectivism over individualism, for example, "does not mean, of course, that a country's Individual Index score tells all there is to be known about the backgrounds and structure of relationship patterns in that country. It is an abstraction that should not be extended beyond its limited area of usefulness."[6]

Osland and Bird reinforce that failing to specify the conditions that lead to high or low measures of a cultural dimension, or not considering other impacts from organizational culture, diminishes rather than enriches our comparative understanding of culture and business practices. These approaches reduce rather than expand opportunities for learning and exploration.

Common cultural dimensions are important, and I would say should serve as a necessary facet of education in any organization's DEI learning. Doing so without an explicit emphasis on sense-making, and what we will share about the other two dimensions of CQ (Strategy and Action), can move from the usefulness of sophisticated stereotypes to dichotomies that Westerners and organizations acculturated by Western norms have a tendency to create. This way of interpreting individuals and groups fails to create space for paradoxes and more complete pictures. Their stereotypes, even those considered sophisticated, wouldn't be wrong per se; they would simply be grossly incomplete and misused. The lack of broader context can lead to a host of challenges, the most harmful being the unconscious systemic exclusion of certain groups when influential individuals or tendencies of the organizational mind perpetuate unnuanced extremes.

These extreme interpretations are increasingly a default for some individuals, organizations, and even within the narrative of geographies and their various humankinds. When it comes to the practice of diversity, equity, and inclusion in organizations, it benefits them to create vehicles to teach people how they can develop the skills to more effectively, and situationally, recognize the nuances of the various constructs that may be predominant in their interpretation of others and themselves.

CQ offers a way to do this. And what is great about the approach of CQ is that it provides a built-in feedback loop that, if used mindfully, can put individuals and their respective organizations in a position to consistently grow their cultural intelligence and agility through working with a variety of people and across any number of business contexts. This evolving skill set creates organizational capability to sustain a culture committed to making DEI normative.

CQ Strategy and Action: Act, Think, Rethink Actions

While it would be nice to think that I've helped my wife, Martina, grow her CQ, the truth is my CQ has improved because of her.

Martina's parents were born in northwestern Spain. They grew up in the region of Galicia, speaking two languages—Galician, which is a combination of Spanish and Portuguese, and Castilian Spanish, which is the primary national language and their second mother tongue. Their cultural values were formed considerably by their upbringing in Spain.

In their late teens and twenties, respectively, my mother-in-law and father-in-law moved to the French-speaking canton (municipality) of Jura in Switzerland. For those unfamiliar, Switzerland has four official languages primarily based on the countries in which it shares borders. My mother-in-law was the pioneer, coming to the country as a young woman with a few technical skills, to work in housekeeping for a hotel. She was followed by my father-in-law, and then, like many immigrant families all over the world, many of Martina's maternal aunts and uncles moved to Jura for work and to create wealth that would allow them to later return to Spain much more prosperous than they could have become working in Spain. Some of them brought their children with them. Others, like Martina, her brother and cousins, and their families, were born and raised in Switzerland.

The Martinez-Gómez families were not the only ones to immigrate to Switzerland. They were preceded and followed by many Gallegos immigrating for similar reasons. In fact, throughout Switzerland, there are approximately thirty thousand of them.

Immigrating to Switzerland, or even being born here, doesn't make one a Swiss citizen as it does in some countries, including the US. Before 1992, dual citizenship was not possible in Switzerland. If you were born in

Switzerland to a non-Swiss, you had to relinquish your parents' nationality to gain a Swiss passport. That has changed, but one can imagine the identity dynamics such a policy could create.

Martina is a non-citizen resident (at the time of this writing) in a country where she was born, raised, has lived in her entire life, and speaks three of the four official languages (along with five other languages spoken in Europe). As an American, not having automatic citizenship seemed bizarre to me when first learning about it. However, she is clear that it was a choice then, and while she didn't act on getting her Swiss citizenship, instead opting for filial piety and not giving up her Spanish nationality inherited at birth (which was a necessary requirement at the time), she considers herself as belonging to both cultures and countries.

Her straddling the culture she was born into along with the more Germanic one she acquired after moving to the German-speaking part of Switzerland in her early twenties gives her a cultural lens for distinctions and an ability to navigate across them like few other people have. And while I feel like my global travels, diverse friendships, vocation, and intrinsic and extrinsic drive and knowledge about cultures have boosted my CQ, what my wife has is a plethora of learned behaviors and a reflexive capacity to prepare for and adjust to situations.

Our interactions as a couple over the years have produced a great deal of comic relief, especially as our vocabularies across the four languages spoken in our home and family overlap. When Martina says to me (what I hear) that she is "working [at] home," I have come to know that she is on her way home on foot instead of on the tram. And when I start to use obscure American slang or vocabulary and she looks at me puzzled (we even speak different English), I can pause and change my word choice more rapidly.

The growth of our relationship has required that we think about our thinking, as one would use metacognitive strategies, and adjust our behaviors when we see misunderstanding emerging. Sometimes she is quite culturally Spanish; other times, she is more Swiss-French or Germanic, and I am increasingly less American, and she appreciates my learning.

The advantages of having high CQ Strategy and Action can close gaps for someone who has high levels of CQ Drive and Knowledge. As David Livermore states, "CQ strategy is the key link between our cultural understanding and behaving in ways that result in effective leadership." And "CQ action is primarily the outcome of our drive, knowledge, and strategy."

I like to use the example of a music producer. Music producers listen very closely. Before they start working with a musician, they begin to consider their current experience with the artist from past live performances, conversation about their musical vision, and many other areas. They think and then rethink what might be possible in co-creation with the artist. They try one configuration, reflect on it along with the artist, and then they try again. Each time, the idea is that they seek to capture the perspectives of all those who will be interacting with the music—the artist(s), the audience, in some cases the record label, and of course themselves. Every engagement is an opportunity to engage in bidirectional, multimodal, and multidimensional learning.

I see CQ Strategy and Action as similar to what renowned Brazilian sociologist and educator Paulo Freire refers to as *praxis*, "reflection and action upon the world in order to transform it." Freire states that many people see dialogue as debate. It is an attempt to be right, to win. The connotation for dialogue for many is an oppressive one of dominance and subordination. True dialogue is transformational. It requires humility. We might even use the term "cultural humility," in this instance. It is a respectful stance that holds the aspiration of understanding—no one wins if the other leaves feeling disrespected or devalued in any capacity.[7]

Such thoughtful practice requires that people know how to reflectively adapt. CQ Action requires a sense of knowing how and when to "flex"—that is, to adjust to the context to produce a win-win situation for all involved. Just as the producer needs to know that flexing will be needed (CQ Strategy), they also need to know when and how to do so, or not to do so, to most effectively create a meaningful musical outcome, together.

Continuing with a Freirean analogy, producers need to be in the stance of the "teacher-student," careful not to overly attach to their "knowing" and impose their views on the artist(s). And if we take ourselves as producers practicing CQ Strategy and Action, other times we will be in dialogue with the artists taking the perspective of "student-teachers" on the views and concerns of all. As Avinash Kumar writes on The Educationist blog, "This confluence of ideas and views would lead to the 'co-creation' of content and new knowledge (for both)."[8]

When I think about my interactions with my former work colleague mentioned earlier, where I missed the mark was that I didn't robustly practice CQ Strategy and Action in a way that gave us the best opportunity to co-create. There was a part of me that wanted to be right. This was not practicing humility, and it was not a reflection of high CQ in the areas I needed it most. I am humbled by the learning.

If you think about your cross-cultural interactions in the past, where could you have benefited from better reflection and adaptation? Consider how you can plan cross-cultural interactions, check your assumptions and plans, adapt your communication style, take a different approach to negotiations, and practice *praxis*.

Implications for Developing an Inclusion System

Skill building in DEI is often built around awareness. But awareness alone is insufficient if the goal is making inclusiveness normative.

> Being aware is important. But creating the conditions for everyone to thrive requires a set of skills and capabilities to move from willingness to skillfulness. CQ is a mechanism for all of us to develop skills and capabilities that we can strive to constantly improve and refine. Thinking about our thinking, or metacognition, is like developing a muscle to be deeply and actively self-reflective.
>
> I recognize that I am not always able to quickly empathize with everyone, even when I would like to. Perspective-taking is a skill set that I have been able to learn and refine as I have deepened my learning in CQ.

Perspective-taking has personally led me to learn about colleagues, understand what they want and why, while simultaneously working to create win-win solutions with them.

Context is constantly changing around here. Our roles, organizational history, tenure, and networks influence how we receive and interpret information and one another. Context can enable or get in the way of us knowing where we each are coming from and how we can move things forward, together. With the skills of CQ, we can come to recognize that values matter and that matters will emerge via values. The better we understand our own cultural values, the more effectively we can determine how values can be supplemental or complementary in our learning with one another.

Our cultural values contain multitudes of exformation (everything we discard when we share a message or information with someone). Refining our CQ, despite disparate exformation, can help us build the skills to make our interactions and exchanges more meaningful and robust. Doing so, along with more refined metacognition and perspective-taking, represents a foundational skill that can help us realize the evergreen goals of our culture: every colleague thriving and generating positive energy for the growth of all of our stakeholders.

—Sincerely, Your CEO

Social Capital: Connection, Reciprocity, Possibility

"Community connectedness is not just about warm fuzzy tales of civic triumph. In measurable and well-documented ways, social capital makes an enormous difference in our lives . . . Social capital makes us smarter, healthier, safer, richer, and better able to govern a just and stable [society]."

—Robert D. Putnam

I f I think back to the people, institutions, and ideas that have shaped my life and my career aspirations, I have to pay homage to the social ties I inherited as a result of the family I was born into, the values instilled, and the networks that those values have led me to be a part of. I also owe much to church elders, like my first pastor, John T. Olds, who I can distinctly remember saying from the pulpit, "let people know not only that you are thankful to them, but that you truly appreciate them." He meant, say this literally and show them with your actions of reciprocity and compassion.

There was also Sister Thelma Hayes, who was the head of the usher board at my home church. She reinforced with the greatest of care what she saw as the gift of serving the congregation on Sunday morning. Under her guidance, we made sure the congregants could find a place to sit and secure a hymnal if one wasn't in its proper place or if they weren't available in sufficient numbers, and we collected the weekly tithes and offering and much more. And it was Brother Richard Stinson who stuttered and was the most attentive listener I have ever met. He always took note of what the youth of the church were saying, and he always had something funny or positive to say in response. Interestingly, he had an absolutely beautiful voice and sang from his heart where no intermittent breaks existed, like in his listening.

Growing up and being a part of institutions such as my church, civic organizations, community athletics, and the broader community in my hometown of Topeka, Kansas, made up my *social capital*. Social capital has been one of the most popular subjects in the social sciences over the past few decades. Hundreds of journal articles and more than one hundred edited volumes and books about and related to the subject have been published since the 1990s.

Naturally, I wasn't familiar with the term growing up, but I did consider these organizations part of my identity, and they have clearly contributed to how I see and engage with the world today. Like financial capital, we all have varying amounts and types of social capital. While there is the capacity for economic sociologists to measure the social capital of an individual or group, the quantity of social capital doesn't necessarily equate to greater fiscal or physical resources. There are some people who have high amounts of certain types of social capital, as we will discuss in this chapter. The volume of one's social capital doesn't necessarily equate to any form of financial benefit. For example, Bob Edwards and Michael W. Foley, longtime academic collaborators on social capital and contemporaries of Robert Putnam (quoted in the opening of this chapter), present the example that having a dense network of connections in a dying industry would be of little value, like having job skills that are relevant to an economically obsolete occupation.[1] While the social capital in this example may be higher, the quality and variety is of little consequence to getting ahead financially.

So what's the point of talking about social capital in a book about diversity, equity, and inclusion? To understand that, we first need to define social capital, which requires looking at a few different perspectives because there's currently no recognized standard definition. In fact, there are some who quasi-reject the term as it is most popularly laid out by Harvard political scientist Robert Putnam in his book *Bowling Alone*.[2] Putnam introduced me to social capital, and he defines it based on the definition of L. J. Hanifan, who was a state supervisor of rural schools in West Virginia back in 1916. His version—and thus Putnam's version—contained commonly agreed upon elements such as goodwill, fellowship, reciprocity, and social and civic engagement among individuals and families who are part of a social unit. Putnam states, "Social capital refers to connections among individuals—social networks and the norms of reciprocity and trustworthiness that arise from them." In that sense, social capital is closely related to what some have called "civic virtue." The difference is that "social capital" calls attention to the fact that civic virtue is most powerful when embedded in a dense network of reciprocal social relations. A community of virtuous isolated individuals is not likely to be rich in social capital.

Author Margaret Heffernan, on the other hand, defines social capital as "the trust, knowledge, reciprocity and shared norms that create quality of life and make a group resilient. In any company, you can have a brilliant bunch of individuals—but what prompts them to share ideas and concerns, contribute to one another's thinking, and warn the group early about potential risks is their connection to one another. Social capital lies at the heart of just cultures: it is what they depend on—and it is what they generate."[3]

What Heffernan articulates is among many organizations' proximate goals for their organizational culture. When I speak with clients, they often tell me that they want a collegial culture where people feel psychologically safe and have a sense of belonging. I aspire to these ideals with them. I am also clear, as Heffernan reinforces, that spending time and creating greater connectivity can lead to gains in innovation and creativity as ideas collide and people have space to safely debate.

Conversely, I also hold another position that makes the active cultivation of social capital in organizations more complex, especially when considering diversity of context, organizational design, and inclusion. As Edwards and Foley state, there is no form of capital that is equally distributed in American society [or in any society]. And the reality is that individuals don't have equal opportunity to access the various forms of capital. Not all forms of human, cultural, or social capital are uniformly valuable as resources for individual or collective action. Thus, a notion of social capital that is inherently benevolent and always helpful is incomplete.

Sociologist James Coleman continues in this vein, stating that certain types of social capital valuable in creating certain actions for some (e.g., small groups with specialized knowledge creating heightened inaccessibility or inequity, intentional creation of in- and out-groups, violent opposition to those considered "other," subversion of certain groups or identities, etc.) may be of no use or potentially harmful to others. In this sense, let's consider groups like the Khmer Rouge, whose leader, Pol Pot, led the genocide of an estimated 2.2 million Cambodians between 1975 and 1979. Those who belonged to the Khmer Rouge and followed Pol Pot benefited from the social capital accumulated from their association and related actions. Obviously, those who were not a part of that group were adversely impacted. Social capital is not a panacea.

There are limitations to social capital's benefits. And without a doubt, the various facets of social capital embedded in social structures can be productive and can make "possible the achievement of certain ends that in its absence would not be possible."[4]

Coleman doesn't look at social capital as something social psychological—that social capital is a simple quality of an individual. Rather, "social capital is a structural category that exists in conjunction with norms and values available as resources to those individuals who share access to a particular social context."[5] This perspective of social capital not being psychologized was reflective of French sociologist Pierre Bourdieu, who defined social capital as "the aggregate of the actual or potential resources which are linked to possession of a durable network of more or less institutionalized relationships of mutual acquaintance and recognition—or in other words, to membership in a group."[6] The amount of social capital possessed by an individual is dependent on the size and configuration of the network of connections one can mobilize and on the volume of capital—economic, cultural, and symbolic—possessed by one's connections.

Bourdieu's and Coleman's definitions and explanation of social capital line up with why and how I see investment and attention to social capital as critical in creating sustainable inclusion and equitable outcomes for everyone who is part of the life of an organization. In my definition, social capital is *the intentionally or unintentionally cultivated network of relationships where the context of the network produces different outcomes.* By definition, like Coleman, it is neutral, but when the context is disparate in terms of access to power and exposure, the results generally lead to network inequities. When we talk about organizational life, social capital is something that is seen as being organically formed. If we are interested in creating actions that allow everyone to thrive and for your organizational culture to be generative, then intentionality is needed to unlock the robustness and value that can be created through organizational networks.

Bonding, Bridging, and Linking

Social capital is not a solution that automatically works for organizations unless it is cultivated intentionally with purpose and thoughtfulness. There are two reasons for company attentiveness when thinking about the development of social capital: first, social capital is neither created nor distributed equally or equitably among the various networks that people and the organizations in which they are embedded inhabit; and second, the different types of social capital have different characteristics.

Let's explore three aspects of social capital and then discuss how these might play out when thinking about making inclusion sustainable in organizational life.

There are distinctions in social capital just as there are distinctions in financial capital. While one wouldn't equate terms like debt and equity to social capital, their equivalent could be bonding and bridging; as well as a third distinction, *linking* social capital, which can be considered a type of bridging social capital. Figure 8 provides a snapshot of the distinction between bonding and bridging social capital based on the literature.[7]

Bonding social capital consists of the social connections within groups where members are similar in demographics, attitudes, beliefs, and information resources.

Bonding Social Capital	Bridging Social Capital
Within	Between
Intra	Inter
Exclusive	Inclusive
Closed	Open
Inward looking	Outward looking
"Getting by"	"Getting ahead"
Horizontal	Vertical
Integration	Linkage
Strong ties	Weak ties
People who are alike	People who are different
Thick trust	Thin trust
Network closure	Structural holes

Distinctions between bonding and bridging social capital

Figure 8

Bonding social capital exists in a construct of people like ourselves (rather than like "others") and who typically have strong, close relationships. Examples include alumni of the same school, family members, close friends, common civic group members, and neighbors. These relationships develop between people of similar backgrounds and interests, and they provide material and emotional support and are more inward-looking and protective. These networks have a high density of connection between members, and most, if not all of them, are interconnected and interact frequently with each other. While friendships are often considered bonding social capital, they can also be bridging ties in that there is more of a propensity for these close ties to provide a friend access to others previously unknown.

While I hold the view that social capital is a neutral form of capital, when enacted, it can provide advantages to one group at the expense of others. In organizations, depending on their size and geographical distribution (time zone proximity; physical distance; and, in larger firms, location of work and meeting spaces), there are varying degrees of bonding. While there is the likelihood of bonding due to being a part of the same organizational umbrella, bonding ties also happen in more discrete parts of the organization such as within disciplines or teams; along the stratification of alumni, corporate, or local affiliations; or even along the lines of hobbies and other common personal interests.

These various mechanisms of bonding social capital aren't objectively good or bad. But when the affinities lead to unfair advantages for exclusive groups of people, inequities are inevitable. For the most part, people don't have an intention to create anything that might exclude or occlude, but the nature of these bonds can make those pitfalls possible. Putnam has suggested that bonding social capital is helpful for "getting by." That is, in a relatively closed network, the inward-looking relationships formed allow one to navigate these spaces more effectively. The more stratification of bonded networks inside of an organization, the more possibility for bias and exclusion there is.[8] What we often see in companies reflects bonding social capital. Of course, looking at the identity of those who seem to be "getting by" better than others, an easy conclusion when their identities don't match one's own is that they are not just getting by, but they are getting ahead of you because of their bondedness. If this is the case, which it too often is, unfair opportunities are often granted by those blinded by their fortune of bondedness—what might be translated as privilege.

This does not mean advocating against bonding social capital because it reinforces privilege. Rather, it means helping people understand the nature of bonding and how it can unintentionally create bottlenecks in the process of true organizational inclusion. This might take on different forms, depending on organizational structure or DEI programming.

One example is employee resource groups (ERGs). Single-identity-focused ERGs are, by their nature, at least in part bonded groups based on their shared history, sentiments, and stories. The benefits of such groups are that they can create a sense of safety for participants to find support during situations that might be difficult to navigate without access to people who have experience in successfully progressing through them. ERGs can be instrumental in creating a sense of belonging among the members of such closed networks.

While mattering to one's in-group has value, it is also possible that in the accumulation of bonding social capital, people can become rooted in their own identities to such an extent that there is little perspective that makes its way in or out to manifest bridging or weak ties to "get ahead." As Putnam says, it is the nature and power of an outward focus that creates links across differences and distinctions. Bonding social capital is characterized by investment in and extraction of value from groups familiar to us.

When we consider dynamics of power, access, and agency, the value of close ties varies across identities. Bonding social capital must be evaluated for how and whom it provides greatest value. I won't attribute a hierarchy of value related to identity in terms of financial or social value. However, when considering the potential of network ties, I do believe it is critical that we recognize the self-imposed limitations (inside of organizations and institutions) of groups bonded to such a degree, often by identity—principally that they miss the opportunity to create the bridging ties that benefit their valued affinities while also providing benefits to their organizations at large.

As I have worked to teach the fundamentals of developing Inclusion Systems to organizations, my focus has primarily been on bridging social capital. Siloed thinking and action in organizations has largely resulted in bonded groups maintaining their monocultures; past success justifies the perpetuation of skewed social capital. Monocultures, as shared in chapter two, inevitably cause serious damage to ecosystems and are unsustainable.

Bridging social capital is a type of social capital characterized by connections across differences that are often divided, such as status, class, caste, race, or religion. It allows groups to share and exchange information across difference, foster ideas and innovation, and build common context where their difference might otherwise have been inhibiting. The "weak ties" of overlapping networks can provide accessibility to resources and opportunities that exist in one network to members of another.[9]

While I've never questioned the value of ERGs, I have had my doubts about whether they are fulfilling all their potential. While multinational companies are in the midst of a global dialogue about racism and white supremacy, there is no doubt that having a safe space to share stories of the personal impact is critical. Simultaneously, if these stories remain inside of bonded groups, without outward actions toward the transformation of the current state, there is a risk that any potential for transformation will be lost to anchoring on the pain of what is and what has been. In building the solidarity needed to shift the horrific remnants of the dehumanization of any oppressed group, building metaphorical and relational bridges is necessary.

Creating bridging and diverse social capital closes structural holes in organizational life.[10] Bridging social capital brings people together, allowing them (without diminishing differences) to create possibilities for inquiry, innovation, ideation, and insights in ways that only a more distant view, enabled by trust and fresh perspectives, can provide.

My recommendation for ERGs (extending to the organizations where they exist) is to *bond with care and bridge with purpose*. The sustainable actions, policies, and structural changes that many people desire for their organizations lie not in how many people from a bonded group join a cause important to the group. Change happens when there is a clear understanding and shared contextual knowledge of how the cause of one group impacts and holds the potential to be transformative for the benefit of everyone.

One other form of capital is *linking* social capital. Linking social capital is seen by some scholars, many of whom are from the World Bank, as an extension of bridging social capital. The distinction is that linking social capital is about connections and relationships fostered between individuals and groups or different levels of social status and hierarchy based on power and wealth.[11] Linking capital is class-oriented more than identity-related.

Power dynamics matter. As we learned in the consideration of power in organizational design and from the work of Dr. Sukhvinder Obhi, power is critical to making organizations function better. It can have a negative impact on both organizational culture and the behaviors that leaders display, leading to a variety of barriers toward change. Power is a key factor in determining progress toward developing an Inclusion System.

Diffusion of Innovations

As we discussed in chapter eight on meritocracy, we know that a substantial amount of advantage that people have isn't cognitive or genetically based. Generational networks, particularly heavily bonded ones, often provide a head start.

The advantage, however, is not fixed. It is primarily about information, how that information is diffused, and who the recipients of that information are. In fact, when it comes to diffusion of ideas leading to innovations, the more similar, or what sociologist and author Everett Rogers notes as the more *homophilous*, one's network is, the harder it is for an innovation to take hold. Rogers says, "This tendency for more effective communication to occur with those who are more similar to a change agent occurs in most diffusion campaigns. Unfortunately, those individuals who most need the help provided by the change agent are least likely to accept it."[12] In other words, in organizational life or entrepreneurship, when one is working to sell a new idea or innovation, it is beneficial to have diffusion that taps into *heterophilous* networks of difference.

Given that every organization with a desire for sustainable growth has a focus on innovation, it's important to couple that desire with an understanding that robust innovation diffusion requires channels characterized by heterophily (network diversity) and that "the diffusion of innovations is a social process, even more than a technical matter."[13] This means that what's important to organizations related to inclusion and difference is of significant value to business standing. It is possible that insufficient attention to how and through whom innovations and ideas flow could unknowingly limit a firm's capacity to move thinking from idea to innovations in the most expedient manner—thus decreasing the probability of adoption within a relevant time span.

I have seen homophily block potential innovations. These innovations were not always fully developed ideas, but they were ideas vetted by a narrowly constructed and often small group of people with perspectives that were based on a fixed set of individual and organizational preferences, traditions, and conveniences.

One example that I came across was from a data scientist working in knowledge management who had experienced that people in their organization struggled to discover complementary expertise across the large global organization. The scientist spoke to many people around the organization in their network and found an overwhelming resonance with the hypothesis of disparate access to internal information and expertise in some of the most important emerging technologies in the industry.

This scientist recognized that the formal structures of the organization were insufficient for cutting-edge ideas to flow through and influence decision-makers. To address this, they discovered an approach to making colleagues' interests and expertise transparent to everyone interested in willing disclosure of their scientific learning and passions beyond their current roles. The data scientist discovered that many people were willing to share the information and did. The hypothesis of a lack of connectivity of emerging expertise and ideas was sound. And despite an initial proof of concept, the data scientist's voice was muted by the louder, more centralized voices in the organizational network.

This didn't leave them discouraged. It led them to be even further inspired by the power of weak ties in advancing innovative ideas that were likely to emerge in the least likely places, including those that occurred as network outliers. The data scientist's project didn't die; it just stayed bundled up in a small fringe group of curious people.

Eventually, some of those ideas like artificial intelligence and machine learning in *in silico* drug design and discovery were adopted into mainstream ways of operating because people with greater hierarchical power finally began to recognize that not having the expertise, identified by the protagonist of this story years earlier, was getting in the way of what they saw as an essential need. By the time the latent idea was brought forward, the opportunity for a competitive edge that the organization could have realized was, at best, diminished. In fact, the organization needed to catch up. The data scientist left the organization for one who appreciated their perspectives and forward thinking.

It is difficult to calculate the loss to the data scientist's old organization for failing to recognize the innovation that was brought to light but met with a lagging response from the central organizational influencers. We don't know if the leadership had a plan to close the gap and catch up with competitors small and large in the then cutting-edge, later clearly necessary, and now mainstream, technologies (e.g., machine learning, artificial intelligence, and quantum computing). I would say that it doesn't matter, because unless the organization invested in the necessary steps to remove impediments in the diffusion of innovations, it would happen repeatedly.

Author Jared Diamond, in talking about the evolution of technologies, says, "Because technology begets more technology, the importance of an invention's diffusion potentially exceeds the importance of the original invention."[14] Existing and advancing technologies are not only the result of a society (or even a company) accumulating its own ideas, but also adopting those of other societies. In the case of the data scientist above, they saw the emerging need for expertise and adoption technologies that were mainly in the realm of computer science, network science, machine learning, and artificial intelligence as they related to solving healthcare challenges. They saw the adjacent possibilities that these advances held before this was widely seen as an absolute necessity. It's safe to say that all of the above are dominating current healthcare strategies and large-scale projects.

Many technological advances and opportunities have been delayed (e.g., clean energy or lab grown/cultured meat) due to current industries, their vested interests, and political influence. Even when a technology is amply diffused, connecting with actors in an organization, society, or related entity, without sufficient adoption/adopters and intentional maintenance, it would be lost. This doesn't mean that the technologies, like clean renewable energy technology, won't eventually find their place in the future. It does suggest that the advantages of early adoption and the velocity that it carries can be unknowingly sacrificed without proper attention to organizational networks. There are few business leaders who wouldn't agree that adoption of an innovation/breakthrough idea to solve an intractable problem earlier is highly advantageous. Even if there is resistance to an idea, having it be adopted by organizational actors that can guide it toward activation ahead of one's competition is a winning strategy.

When I talked about exclusion in chapter ten, I suggested that leaving out someone or something from communication critical to their work is predominantly unintentional. Nonetheless, our frequent failures to articulate information based on the needs of the audience quickly create a sense of distrust. Whether one believes in diversity, equity, and inclusion conceptionally or not, we can reasonably agree that trust is critical business glue for all stakeholders in your networks.

Every organizational and social network has a limited number of highly trusted opinion leaders. In the formal structures of organizations, this trust factor is not necessarily dependent on positions of power in the hierarchy. In fact, positional leaders in the organizational hierarchy might be less trusted based on organizational and individual context (often because of perceptions of them not caring or being open, or not being safe to approach). Knowing where trusted opinion leaders lie in your informal networks is critical to innovation and culture. The challenge is how to do so and, once you do, how to act to make sure that those opinion leaders encounter innovators and have the space to explore ideas together. At least so they stay motivated and don't leave for a firm that will assure such connections frequently occur.

Rogers suggests that innovation decisions in a diverse, heterophilous system go through a five-step process by which an innovation is communicated via various channels. These five steps consist of:[15]

1. *Knowledge* is gained when an individual learns about an innovation and begins to understand how it functions.
2. *Persuasion* occurs once one forms a favorable or less than favorable attitude toward the innovation.
3. *Decision* happens when an individual does things (with others) that lead to a choice of adopting or rejecting the innovation.
4. *Implementation* takes place when the innovation is used. Here the innovation can morph through reinvention.
5. *Confirmation* is when reinforcement is sought after in order to solidify the decision. In this phase, the innovation is not guaranteed as disconfirming information can come from an opinion leader's network, causing rejection.

Diffusion's importance to my central question of how we make inclusion accessible, actionable, and sustainable lies in the fact that it occurs within a social system. A social system consists of the interrelated units engaged in joint problem solving.

Social structures of ideas and innovation affect diffusion. The influence of leaders and change agents and the kinds of decisions and consequences of an innovation ecosystem (norms of diffusion) are affected by social structure, and thus they constantly change with context. The social structure is made up of the orientation and distinctions in the relationships of an organization and how ideas move through it.

This means that social structures, which provide regularity and stability to human behavior (in an organization), can, to an extent, semi-accurately help predict behavior. The predictive aspects of social structures can lead to people being manipulated, as we have seen emerge in the tech sphere, especially across social media platforms. In organizational life, such manipulation can occur as well. Attention to organizational networks, and how information flows (from individual to individual, team to team, department to department, collaborator), holds the potential to shift from an in-group-favored and often inequitably distributed few into a cornucopia of insights from a broad array of perspectives, interests, and possibilities. My hope is that, rather than manipulation, predictive behavior on how ideas and innovations move through networks serves a purpose that broadly benefits organizations.

Intentionality in the cultivation of and inquiry into organizational networks and social structures opens up many possibilities for organizational life.

Sociological diffusion happens via social structures. In the natural sciences, diffusion is the net movement of something (a molecule, atom, or ion) from a space of higher concentration to one of lower concentration. Diffusion happens across what is called a concentration gradient. Consider that all organizations have a metaphorical concentration gradient. And now think about the notion that some organizations also exist as a collection of closed systems where such gradients are within those systems, be they departments, disciplines, levels of seniority, or what have you. Diffusion might happen at varying rates within those closed systems, but diffusion naturally happens over time.

Now, consider how much energy is needed for diffusion inside those closed systems as compared to willingly fostering openness that allows diffusion to happen across systems. If you have been in a large organization or

have watched your organization grow over time from one where size and
necessity made diffusion fast to one that (mostly unintentionally) resulted
in the emergence of a series of closed systems, you can relate to how difficult robust information sharing (including innovations) can be. This challenge and energy output is not due to a lack of desire. It is more likely
due to a lack of awareness, attention, and action in the cultivation of your
organizational networks.

Why You Need a Head of Social Capital

If your first reaction to this heading was, "Whoa! Amri, you are asking us
to create a new role just to manage this social capital stuff?," my answer
would be the German word *Yein*, which means "yes and no." Yes, you need
a Head(s) of Social Capital. No, you don't necessarily need to create new
head count. In fact, you likely have people who are already quite masterful
at cultivating social capital in their current roles. Now, you must identify one
or more of these colleagues and create space for them to spend quality time
attending to social capital.

Organizations spend considerable time attending to financial capital
and human capital. They feel these to be necessary for optimal human-
organizational functioning. The prioritization of the two varies from organization to organization depending on the structures and prevailing values
of the firm. Few organizations spend relative and complementary time
attending to social capital. I don't think this lack of attention is a result of
not wanting to, but more so a lack of recognition of how important it is and
how a modest investment can boost the two other forms of capital, as well
as provide other benefits to the organization.

Creating a role(s) focused on social capital, at the very least, allows for
exploration and experimentation around how your organization bridges
across departments, disciplines, locations, links between hierarchical levels, and creates channels of engagements with external stakeholders. These
insights might inform how teams are formed, how a product is launched,

and/or simply tell you how people are faring amid the rapid pace of change that we are experiencing as "normal" in all ways except having a full understanding of the impact.

I recommend the role of Head of Social Capital include the following as part of their responsibilities:

1. **Know your data:** Use organizational network analysis to understand informal organizational structures.
2. **Bridge and link:** Connect areas of networks that could benefit (e.g., innovators to influencers) from greater connectivity with one another. Mentoring is one way to create bridging ties organization-wide.
3. **Educate:** Create mechanisms to help people become more aware of (tangible) opportunities for their growth and development.
4. **Illuminate:** Dive into the tensions of disparate connections. In this exploration, structural barriers can be revealed and addressed.
5. **Tell stories:** Communicate the narratives of connectivity. Share narratives about how connection is enabling the organizational mission and about the opportunities that have yet to be explored.

A Head of Social Capital's role description can include and go far beyond these succinct responsibilities. In fact, if an organization is determined to be purpose-driven and inclusive, it would naturally benefit from investing in social capital. The role may even be part of the DEI leader's team or the leader themself.

The more I learn about social capital, the more I believe that relationships with stakeholders across a spectrum of influence and impacts is what allows us to fulfill our purpose. Attending to and understanding our social capital is another signal of our prioritization of inclusion. In my opinion, doing so is one of the most viable mechanisms to address structural and behavioral inclusion simultaneously and in a manner that is sustainable.

Part of our strategy in the development of our Inclusion System will be to invest in our capacity to do organizational network analysis (ONA) and use what we learn to develop the right inputs, address any inequities discovered, and capitalize on opportunities revealed by the data. I recognize that our organization is more dispersed than ever—COVID-19 has made that reality even clearer. Without intending to, the increased dispersion has likely led to some being and feeling left out and it has left us blind to what people need to contribute at their best during these changing times.

I believe the power of being attentive to social capital, and the act of collecting the right data and doing robust sense-making about our findings, will generate returns that will positively influence all dimensions of organizational life and lead to organizational flourishing. My intention is for all of us to be active social capitalists in some way (e.g., mentoring across different or individual participation/membership in ERGs whose attributes differ from the majority), shape, or form. Doing so will go a long way toward the interdependence critical to making inclusion normative.

—Sincerely, Your CEO

Conclusion

"It doesn't matter what it is. What matters is what it will become."

—**Dr. Seuss**

E arly in this text I asked the following questions: What are we trying to create with DEI? If representation increases, what do we do next? If we focus on retention and the numbers stay the same, what do we do next? If the numbers go up, what do we do next? If our organizational climate/engagement survey data say, "we are an inclusive organization now," then what do we do next?

My answer is deconstruction, followed by reconstruction. Reconstructing and deconstructing DEI is not a standalone idea, nor a time-limited reaction to current events. It is the cultivation of mindsets and skill sets purposed to help stakeholders in your organization discover and constantly reimagine how to create the conditions for everyone to thrive.

In part one, I deconstructed the framing of some common DEI practices. My intention was to initiate a dialogue that DEI champions, supporters, and, most importantly, practitioners have rarely brought to fruition. We need to mindfully examine our methods and motives, perhaps more than ever. The expansion of the field and the opportunity we have to elevate our practice is once in a generation. We must be dilligent in questioning our rhetoric during this time of expansion brought forth by a global pandemic and worldwide racial tensions.

Our methods require scrutinizing for risk and benefit. Are the data we use to justify a business case for DEI truly viable? Or are we just parroting credible, yet self-interested sources and coming to conclusions with sparse evidence or convenient methodologies? Is our curiosity moving our organizations and clients to measure the long-term impacts of our inputs?

My examination of these and other questions is not about me or my preferences or opinions alone. The intention is to encourage us to center on something bigger than ourselves and our identities. That means choosing humanity. I firmly believe that the work of DEI can redirect us beyond our tribal instincts. The reflex toward the familiar won't disappear because of well-meaning DEI supporters and practitioners propagating our wares in organizational life. Deeper into unexplored motivations and mindsets we must go to unlearn such reflexes.

Part two of the book was about engaging in developing mechanisms whereby the complex adaptive systems (organizations) we are a part of shift toward *making DEI accessible to everyone*. Reconstruction means rethinking language, practices, learning, and data that are gathered and shared and made sense of, together. We have to make room for and welcome critics of the work. We must encourage supporters to probe the why, how, and what of our practices. Reconstructing inclusion requires truth, and it doesn't matter from whom or where it comes.

DEI's role in creating magnetic organizational cultures must come with *unambiguous prioritization*. Actions in the name of DEI include intentional unlearning and relearning (concepts such as othering, meritocracy, intersectionality, and exclusion). Building an Inclusion System calls for us to design our organizations with an inclusive lens and build skills to work across distinctions, cultures, and values. Inclusion Systems see collecting data about our informal networks as a critical requirement in identifying communication/collaboration bottlenecks and overload; identifying less visible, highly impactful colleagues; and identifying opportunities to explore how your network diversity is positioning you for current and future success (or isn't). Additionally, the skills acquired through growing your cultural intelligence are invaluable in building capabilities into the organizational mind to navigate the tensions and complexities of difference and similarity.

Creating an Inclusion System means fostering interdependence. Essential to this system is that it can only operate when engaged with other organizational systems. This means that Inclusion Systems foster interdependence among colleagues and in all areas of your business. Your Inclusion System serves to inform and influence other organizational systems (e.g., talent, marketing, operations, and environmental), and those systems in turn serve as vehicles for sustaining your DEI efforts—making equitable and inclusive behaviors and policies normative.

Inclusion Systems adapt to meet the constantly changing needs of the organization. Skilled practitioners operate your Inclusion System. They cannot do so alone, and everyone must build their capabilities, constantly evaluate, unlearn/learn, and tell stories about how the behavioral, structural, and systemic learning and actions are helping all stakeholders to thrive and the culture to be generative. Generative cultures only exist when inclusion is in play. The probability for their sustainability comes as more colleagues build their capabilities in the DEI space.

DEI efforts also must be united with your organizational raison d'être. Purpose, like DEI, goes beyond statements; it is a way of being and the ultimate employee value proposition. Purpose strengthens companies in ways that short-term high financial returns cannot. When business slows down, purpose ignites the fire toward forging new customer relationships, lines of business, and deepening business with existing customers. At times when a company is doing exceptionally well, purpose keeps stakeholders focused on what matters beyond short-term gains. Purpose creates sustainability. Inclusion Systems require sustainability and therefore they are always aligned with organizational purpose. When I started framing the ideas in the text, I was interested in creating a space for convergence. A common center, like that of a labyrinth or the Ubuntu-inspired image on the cover of the book.

The idea was that DEI supporters, naysayers, and those on the fence could enter into dialogue, not to see who or what is right. (Single-minded pursuits to be right have never transformed anything.) Rather, to recognize that Ubuntu, "I am because we are," is our truth. I challenge you to take my offering in this book as an invitation to continue the journey, to "ease on down the road."

Our polarities and differences of opinion, perspectives about organizational purpose, how we live our values, and the responsibility we have as individuals to create a more equitable society will persist. In fact, they should. Most of what we encounter in the complexity of our organizations, communities, and countries requires the diversity of responses that typically emerge. Some perspectives will resonate with you; others will not. And there is a caveat. Inhumane, compassionless, cold-blooded treatment is never acceptable. If it is detected, even the slightest scent of it must be swiftly dealt with.

My hope and aim has been and continues to be opening up possibilities to build DEI with a conversation for our collective advancement—a dialogue with fellow practitioners, clients, advocates, and adversaries to explore the realities of our interdependence—familial, civic, planetary.

Since the book's early framing, the world has changed. The evidence for our indivisibility has been amplified. To fail to acknowledge it is to be in denial. To be in denial is futile. I am convinced by the convictions of the countless inspirational and influential people I have encountered and observed that there is momentum toward inclusivity and equity serving as essential structural elements toward sustainable organizational and institutional thriving.

My conviction, which I was questioning as I began my writing, has reinforced the magnanimity, integrity, and vision for uplifting the humanity of all toward the greater good without compromise. Our collective minds can align with an intention—to stand for the world we envision for our children and future generations. A world where a global citizenry recognizes that there is no viable or sustainable do-it-yourself strategy. In the quest for inclusive and equitable organizations and communities where their stakeholders exist, we all win or we all lose, as we are all part of the superset that is *humanity*.

I know that it is impossible to return all the grace that the universe has bestowed upon me. I will just keep choosing humanity and trust that doing so resonates in enough hearts to make a meaningful difference toward our transformation.

We can all win together. It's the only way we will.

Acknowledgments

Many of my friends and colleagues have helped shape, challenge, and validate the ideas of this book before and during my writing it. Special thanks go to Jennifer Barnick, who never stopped coaching and helping me develop greater clarity of the vision. To Herb Schaffner, my guide in this publishing process and one of the early editors. Elena Sudakova edited one of the final drafts for accessibility to non-native English speakers. My dear friends and colleagues Stacy Lewis, Yvonne Wolf, Howie Schafer, Argentina Afecion, and Rachel Schafer nudged, challenged, and encouraged me in our many conversations and daily work together as the book emerged. And my editors at BenBella/Matt Holt, Gregory Newton Brown, who helped me polish and fine-tuned several drafts, and Katie Dickman, who moved it to the finish line.

Writing a book takes time and not just when writing it. My mind traveled a lot, even when physically present during the writing process. My dear family was with me from its inception. Thanks for always believing in me and creating the space to follow my passion to my wife, Martina Gómez, step twins Romy and Rafael Elsener, my son Kai Amri, niece Jazmine, my mother Harriett, and my in-laws Delores Martinez and Serafin Gómez.

Amri B. Johnson
Basel-Stadt, Switzerland
April 8, 2022

Endnotes

Introduction

1. Maslow, A.H. (1943). "A Theory of Human Motivation". In *Psychological Review*, 50 (4), 430–437.
2. Blackstock, C. (2011) The Emergence of the Breath of Life Theory. *Journal of Social Work Values and Ethics*, Volume 8, Number 1 (2011) Copyright 2011, White Hat Communications.
3. *Factfulness*, by Hans Rosling: The term "developing world" is a complete misnomer. Rosling suggests that the term makes assumptions about all people in a country and it also can create the belief that some people in lower income countries are less well-off or less happy than those with higher incomes. This is also not true.
4. Quincy Jones and Michael Jackson made the multiplatinum albums *Off The Wall* (1979), *Thriller* (1982), and *Bad* (1987) together over a decade.
5. Harold Arlen—Biography—*We're Off to See the Wizard*. Accessed January 10, 2022. http://www.haroldarlen.com/bio-6.html.
6. Ray, Charles. "'Oz' Family Apologizes for Racist Editorials." NPR. August 17, 2006. Accessed January 10, 2022. https://www.npr.org/templates/story/story.php?storyId=5662524&t=1565458584299.

Chapter 1

1. Norton, Michael I., and Samuel R. Sommers. "Whites See Racism as a Zero-Sum Game That They Are Now Losing." *Perspectives on Psychological Science* 6, no. 3 (May 2011): 215–218.

Chapter 2

1. Michaels, Walter Benn. *The Trouble with Diversity: How We Learned to Love Identity and Ignore Inequality*. Picador, 2016.

2. "Getting Serious About Diversity: Enough Already with the Business Case." *Harvard Business Review*. August 27, 2021. Accessed January 10, 2022. https://hbr.org/2020/11/getting-serious-about-diversity-enough-already-with-the-business-case.

3. "Sidetracked: Why Our Decisions Get Derailed and How We Can Stick to the Plan." Harvard Business School. Accessed January 10, 2022. http://www.hbs.edu/faculty/product/43035.

4. Panzarino, Matthew. "Apple Diversity Head Denise Young Smith Apologizes for Controversial Choice of Words at Summit." TechCrunch. October 14, 2017. Accessed January 10, 2022. https://techcrunch.com/2017/10/13/apple-diversity-head-denise-young-smith-apologizes-for-controversial-choice-of-words-at-summit/.

5. As of July 2018, the US Bureau of the Census estimates that White Americans are the racial majority. African Americans are the largest racial minority, comprising an estimated 13.4 percent of the population. Hispanic and Latino Americans are the largest ethnic minority, comprising an estimated 18.3 percent of the population. The White, non-Hispanic, or Latino population make up 60.4 percent of the nation's total, with the total White population (including White Hispanics and Latinos) being 76.9 percent.

6. There is a growing body of research from the health and social services sector in Australia on "Workforce Mutuality." In some industries matching the workforce population to that of society could yield better outcomes. https://healthwest.org.au/wp-content/uploads/2020/08/Workforce-Mutuality-Standards-2020.pdf.

7. "Back to the Roots Part II—the Roots of the Cavendish Banana in England." Bananaroots. April 11, 2016. https://bananaroots.wordpress.com/2016/04/11/back-to-the-roots-part-ii-the-roots-of-the-cavendish-banana-in-england/.

8. Christensen, Clayton M. *The Innovators Dilemma: When New Technologies Cause Great Firms to Fail*. Boston: Harvard Business Review Press, 2016.

9. Dobbin, Frank, and Alexandra Kalev. 2018. "Why Diversity Training Doesn't Work: The Challenge for Industry and Academia". *Anthropology Now* 10 (2): 48–55.

10. Dyer, Jeff, Hal B. Gregersen, and Clayton M. Christensen. *The Innovators DNA: Mastering the Five Skills of Disruptive Innovators*. Boston: Harvard Business Review Press, 2011.

11. Reed, Touré F. *Toward Freedom: The Case against Race Reductionism*. London: Verso, 2020.

Chapter 3

1. Beck, Lia. "The Rachel Dolezal Netflix Documentary Will Make You So Uncomfortable & That's Exactly What The Director Wants." *Bustle.* April 26, 2018. https://www.bustle.com/p/the-rachel-dolezal-netflix-documentary-will-make -you-so-uncomfortable-thats-exactly-what-the-director-wants-8882750.
2. Rogers, Richard A. (2006-11-01). "From Cultural Exchange to Transculturation: A Review and Reconceptualisation of Cultural Appropriation." *Communication Theory.* 16 (4): 474–503.
3. Described by author, Eckhart Tolle as "the dark shadow cast by the ego, [that] is actually afraid of the light of your [conscience]" Tolle, Eckhart. *The Power of Now: A Guide to Spiritual Enlightenment.* Sydney, NSW: Hachette Australia, 2018.
4. Jr., Henry Louis Gates. "Exactly How 'Black' Is Black America?" *The Root.* February 11, 2013. https://www.theroot.com/exactly-how-black-is-black-america -1790895185.
5. Arceneaux, Michael. "Okay, So About That Rachel Dolezal Documentary." *Essence.* May 31, 2018. https://www.essence.com/entertainment/rachel-dolezal -documentary-netflix-op-ed/.
6. Padawer, Ruth. "Sigrid Johnson Was Black. A DNA Test Said She Wasn't." *New York Times Magazine.* November 19, 2018. https://www.nytimes.com/2018/11/19 /magazine/dna-test-black-family.html.
7. Senge, P. M.. *The Fifth Discipline: The Art and Practice of the Learning Organization* (Revised and Updated Edition). New York: Doubleday. 2006.
8. Freire, Paulo, Myra Bergman. Ramos, Donaldo P. Macedo, and Ira Shor. *Pedagogy of the Oppressed.* New York, NY, USA: Bloomsbury Academic, 2020.
9. Arnold, Ross & Wade, Jon. (2015). A Definition of Systems Thinking: A Systems Approach. *Procedia Computer Science.* 44. 669–678.
10. Hyter, Michael, and Judith L. Turnock. *The Power of Inclusion: Unlock the Potential and Productivity of Your Workforce.* Ontario: Wiley, 2006.
11. United Nations Department of Economic and Social Affairs site, "The 17 Goals," https://sdgs.un.org/goals.
12. Page, Scott E. (2010-11-08). *Diversity and Complexity (Primers in Complex Systems).* Princeton University Press, Kindle Edition, 2010, p. 11.
13. Hesse, Monica. "Perspective | So, What Should We Do with the Kyle Kashuvs of This World?" *Washington Post.* June 19, 2019. https://www.washingtonpost .com/lifestyle/style/so-what-should-we-do-with-the-kyle-kashuvs-of-this-world /2019/06/19/b4743e9a-91e0-11e9-b570-6416efdc0803_story.html.
14. "How to Facilitate Productive CQ Conversations—Cultural Intelligence Center." Cultural Intelligence Center—We Provide Research-based, Innovative Solutions

for Assessing, Predicting, and Improving Cultural Intelligence (CQ). March 19, 2019. https://culturalq.com/blog/how-to-facilitate-productive-cq-conversations/.

Chapter 4

1. Buolamwini, Joy. "InCoding—In The Beginning Was The Coded Gaze." Medium. September 13, 2019. https://medium.com/mit-media-lab/incoding-in-the-beginning-4e2a5c51a45d.
2. Buolamwini, "InCoding."
3. "Trust in Facebook Has Dropped by 66 Percent since the Cambridge Analytica Scandal." NBCNews.com. April 18, 2018. https://www.nbcnews.com/business/consumer/trust-facebook-has-dropped-51-percent-cambridge-analytica-scandal-n867011.
4. "Algorithms of Oppression: How Search Engines Reinforce . . ." https://pubmed.ncbi.nlm.nih.gov/34709921/.
5. Cameron, J., Hurd, G. A., Schwarzenegger, A., Biehn, M., Hamilton, L., Winfield, P., Henriksen, L., . . . MGM Home Entertainment Inc. (2004). *The Terminator*. Santa Monica, CA: MGM DVD.
6. B. Smith and G. Linden, "Two Decades of Recommender Systems at Amazon.com" in *IEEE Internet Computing*, vol. 21, no. 03, pp. 12–18, 2017. doi: 10.1109/MIC.2017.72
7. "How the Twitter Algorithm Works in 2021 and How to Make It Work for You." Social Media Marketing & Management Dashboard. October 26, 2021. https://blog.hootsuite.com/twitter-algorithm/.

Chapter 5

1. Innovation, Diversity, and Market Growth. The Center for Talent Innovation, 2013
2. Thomas, R. Roosevelt. *World Class Diversity Management: A Strategic Approach*. San Francisco, CA: Berrett-Koehler, 2010.
3. Thomas, R. Roosevelt. *Beyond Race and Gender: Unleashing the Power of Your Total Work Force by Managing Diversity*. Publisher Not Identified, 1992.
4. Dobbin, Frank, and Alexandra Kalev. 2017. "Are Diversity Programs Merely Ceremonial? Evidence-Free Institutionalization." 808–828 in *The Sage Handbook of Organizational Institutionalism*, edited by Royston Greenwood, Christine Oliver, Thomas B. Lawrence, and Renate E. Meyer. London: Sage.

5. McKinsey & Co, "Delivering through Diversity" https://www.mckinsey.com /business-functions/organization/our-insights/delivering-through-diversity. Accessed July 2019.

6. https://www.iso.org/obp/ui/#iso:std:iso:30415:ed-1:v1:en

7. Thomas, R. Roosevelt. *Beyond Race and Gender: Unleashing the Power of Your Total Work Force by Managing Diversity.* Publisher Not Identified, 1992.

Chapter 6

1. Young, Heike. "9 Thought-Provoking Quotes About Work-Life Balance." *Forbes,* July 31, 2015. https://www.forbes.com/sites/salesforce/2015/07/31/9-thought -provoking-quotes-about-work-life-balance/?sh=f41aebf309e5.

2. The Deming Institute, Quotes page, https://deming.org/quotes?_sf_s=system& sf_paged=2.

3. Taleb, N. N. (2012). *Antifragile: Things that gain from disorder.* New York: Random House.

4. Adapted from the work of Dr. R. Roosevelt Thomas, Jr.

5. In classical versions of the SDLC, "Planning" would precede "Analysis"; and, Integration & Testing and Operations & Maintenance would respectively precede and follow 'Implementation'. We collapse planning with analysis, assuming a willingness to reconstruct the Inclusion System currently in place. Integration & Testing, Operations & Maintenance are part of what we label as Implementation & Refinement.

6. Diamond, Michael. (2008). Telling Them What They Know: Organizational Change, Defensive Resistance, and the Unthought Known. *Journal of Applied Behavioral Science.* 44. 348–364. 10.1177/0021886308317403.

7. Thomas, R. Roosevelt. *World Class Diversity Management: A Strategic Approach.* San Francisco, CA: Berrett-Koehler, 2010.

8. Block, Peter, and Janis Nowlan. *Flawless Consulting: A Guide to Getting Your Expertise Used.* San Francisco: Jossey-Bass, 2015.

Chapter 7

1. Marley wrote this song amid the turmoil of the Jamaican elections in December 1976, remembered as some of the most violent times in the country. Marley had supported Michael Manley when he won the election in 1972 and became Prime Minister of Jamaica, but four years later—when Marley was by far the most

popular person in Jamaica—he refused to take a political stance as the country was divided between Manley's People's National Party (PNP) and the Jamaica Labour Party (JLP) headed by Edward Seaga. Marley tried to stay politically neutral while offering peace and shelter however he could. Of course, both parties tried to have Marley on their side, especially Manley who was the sitting Prime Minister at the time and tried to regain Marley's support.

2. White, Timothy. *Catch a Fire*, Bob Marley. Höfen: Hannibal, 2009.
3. Kelly, L. M., & Cordeiro, M. (2020). "Three principles of pragmatism for research on Organizational Processes." *Methodological Innovations*, 13(2), 205979912093724. https://doi.org/10.1177/2059799120937242
4. Edmans, Alex. *Grow the Pie How Great Companies Deliver Both Purpose and Profit.* Cambridge University Press, 2022.
5. McDonald, Danny. "Group behind Last Year's Straight Pride Parade Plans pro-Police Boston Rally for Saturday." *Boston Globe*, June 26, 2020. https://www.bostonglobe.com/2020/06/26/metro/group-behind-last-years-straight-pride-parade-plans-pro-police-boston-rally-saturday/.
6. Gergen, Kenneth J. "Social Constructionism and the Transformation of Identity Politics, Draft copy for Newman and Holzman (Eds.). *End of Knowing: A new developmental way of learning.* New York: Routledge, 1999.
7. "Two Arrested in Killings of Trans Women in Puerto Rico." *ADVOCATE*, May 1, 2020. https://www.advocate.com/crime/2020/5/01/two-arrested-killings-trans-women-puerto-rico.

Chapter 8

1. Young, Michael Dunlop. *The Rise of the Meritocracy*. London: Routledge, 2017.
2. Campbell, Joseph. *Occidental Mythology*. London: Souvenir, 2001
3. Castilla, E. J., & Benard, S. "The Paradox of Meritocracy in Organizations." *Administrative Science Quarterly*, 55(4), 543–676. 2010.
4. "Comment: Down with Meritocracy." *The Guardian*, June 29, 2001. https://www.theguardian.com/politics/2001/jun/29/comment.
5. Appiah, Kwame Anthony. "The Red Baron." *The New York Review of Books*, July 2, 2020. https://www.nybooks.com/articles/2018/10/11/michael-young-red-baron/.
6. Wikipedia contributors. (2019, September 18). Liebig's law of the minimum. In Wikipedia, The Free Encyclopedia. Retrieved 14:12, December 4, 2019, from https://tinyurl.com/tva4cdj
7. Hyter, Mike. "Meritocracy: responding to the myth." *Handbook of Business Strategy* 5(1), 41–44, 2004, 10.1108/10775730410494224.

8. Ladyshewsky, Richard K. "Peer Coaching as a Strategy to Increase Learning and Development in Organisational Life—A Perspective." *International Journal of Evidence Based Coaching and Mentoring*. Oxford Brookes University, January 1, 1970. https://radar.brookes.ac.uk/radar/items/26da9f5c-0271-439c-8437-2fa7afe5823d/1/.

Chapter 9

1. Crenshaw, Kimberlé. "Demarginalizing the Intersection of Race and Sex: A Black Feminist Critique of Antidiscrimination Doctrine, Feminist Theory and Antiracist Politics," *University of Chicago Legal Forum*: Vol. 1989: Iss. 1, Article 8.
2. Coaston, Jane. "The Intersectionality Wars." *Vox*, May 20, 2019. https://www.vox.com/the-highlight/2019/5/20/18542843/intersectionality-conservatism-law-race-gender-discrimination.
3. Livermore, David A. *Driven by Difference: How Great Companies Fuel Innovation through Diversity*. New York: AMACOM, American Management Association, 2016.
4. French, David. "Intersectionality, the Dangerous Faith." *National Review*, March 7, 2018. https://www.nationalreview.com/2018/03/intersectionality-the-dangerous-faith/.
5. Collins, P. H. "Intersectionality's definitional dilemmas." *Annual Review of Sociology*, 41, 1–20. 2015.
6. "Intersectionality Score Calculator." Intersectionality Score Calculator | #IntersectionalityScore | @WhatsMyIntScore. https://intersectionalityscore.com/.
7. Schön, Donald A. *Reflective Practitioner*. Taylor and Francis, 2017.

Chapter 10

1. James, William. *The Principles of Psychology*: Vol. 1–2. London, 1890.
2. "Racism Ruins Lives—Hummedia.manchester.ac.uk." https://hummedia.manchester.ac.uk/institutes/code/research/projects/racism-at-work/tuc-full-report.pdf.
3. The Oxford English Dictionary, 2nd edition, Oxford: Clarendon Press. 1989.
4. Rowe, M. Micro-affirmations and micro-inequities. *Journal of the International Ombudsman Association*, 1, 45–48, 2008.
5. Poushter, Jacob, and Kent, Nicholas. "The Global Divide on Homosexuality Persists." *Pew Research Center*, June 25, 2020, https://www.pewresearch.org/global/2020/06/25/global-divide-on-homosexuality-persists/.

6. OED. See also, Merrian-Webster Collegiate Dictionary, Longman Dictionary of Contemporary English.

7. Gómez, María Mercedes. 2006. *Discrimination and Exclusion: Toward an Interdisciplinary Approach to Hate Crimes Law.* Doctoral Dissertation. New School for Social Research, New York City.

8. Yoshino, Kenji. *Covering: The Hidden Assault on Our Civil Rights.* New York: Random House, 2006.

9. Jameel, Maryam, and Joe Yerardi. "Workplace Discrimination Is Illegal, But Our Data Shows It's Still a Huge Problem." *Vox*, February 28, 2019. https://www.vox.com/policy-and-politics/2019/2/28/18241973/workplace -discrimination-cpi-investigation-eeoc.

10. "Racism Ruins Lives—Hummedia.manchester.ac.uk." https://hummedia .manchester.ac.uk/institutes/code/research/projects/racism-at-work/tuc-full -report.pdf.

11. Merriam-Webster Dictionary. https://www.merriam-webster.com/dictionary /ostracism

12. "Anti Bullying Day 2013." Anti Bullying Day 2013 | Nova Scotia Health Authority—Corporate. https://cdha.nshealth.ca/media-centre/video/anti-bullying -day-2013.

13. Williams, K. D. Ostracism: A temporal need-threat model. In M. P. Zanna (Ed.), *Advances in experimental social psychology*, Vol. 41 (275–314). Elsevier Academic Press. https://doi.org/10.1016/S0065-2601(08)00406-1. 2009.

14. Williams, K. D., Cheung, C. K. T., & Choi, W. "Cyberostracism: Effects of being ignored over the Internet." *Journal of Personality and Social Psychology*, 79, 748–762. 2000.

15. Eisenberger, Naomi & Lieberman, Matthew & Williams, Kipling. "Does Rejection Hurt? An fMRI Study of Social Exclusion." *Science* (New York). 302. 290–2. 10.1126. 2003.

16. Keysers, C., & Gazzola, V. The vicarious brain. In M. Mikulincer & P. R. Shaver (Eds.), Mechanisms of social connection: From brain to group (pp. 71–88). American Psychological Association. https://doi.org/10.1037/14250-005. 2014.

17. Bandura, Albert. *Social Foundations of Thought and Action: A Social Cognitive Theory.* Englewood Cliffs, NJ: Prentice Hall, 1995.

18. U Got the Look. Prince. *Sign o' the Times* [Studio Album]

19. Nørretranders, Tor. *The User Illusion: Cutting Consciousness down to Size.* New York: Penguin Books, 1999.

20. Nørretranders, p. 292

21. Laleman, Francis; Supreeth, George. *resourceful exformation: some thoughts on the development of resourcefulness in humans (learning beyond borders)*. Kindle Locations 154–156). Learning Beyond Borders Publishing. Kindle Edition.

Chapter 11

1. Galbraith, Jay R. *Designing Organizations*. Wiley, 2014, Kindle Edition, p. 37.

2. Robert S. Kaplan and David P. Norton, *The Strategy-Focused Organization*, Harvard Business School Press, 2001

3. Actually, I think if free coffee was taken away at many organizations, many people would be more upset than if the DEI office was defunded or diminished.

4. Weissmark, Mona Sue. *The Science of Diversity*. New York: Oxford University Press, 2020.

5. Fritz, Robert. *The Path of Least Resistance: Learning to Become the Creative Force in Your Own Life*. Kent: Elsevier Science, 2014.

6. If you know CDO to stand for something else, it does (or did or never has depending on where you work). In some cases the role of the Chief Diversity Officer (aka CDO) has changed to Chief Inclusion and Equity Officer (CIEO?) or the Chief Inclusion and Belonging Officer (CIBO). The rise of "digital" in organizations might be a call to transform and restructure Diversity offices, too.

7. Ng AH, Steele JR, Sasaki JY, Sakamoto Y and Williams A. Culture moderates the relationship between interdependence and face recognition. *Front. Psychol.* 6:1620. doi: 10.3389/fpsyg.2015.01620. 2015.

8. Schein, Edgar H. *Helping: How to Offer, Give, and Receive Help*. San Francisco: Berrett-Koehler Pub, 2009.

9. Fritz, Robert. *Path of Least Resistance*. Newfane Press. Kindle Edition, 2010.

10. Rainie, Lee and Janna Anderson, "Code-Dependent: Pros and Cons of the Algorithm Age." Pew Research Center, 2017

Chapter 12

1. Ang & Van Dyne. *Handbook of Cultural Intelligence*. ME Sharpe, 2008.

2. Sternberg, R. J.; Detterman, Douglas K., eds. *What is intelligence? Contemporary Viewpoints on its Nature and Definition*. Norwood (NJ): Ablex. 1986.

3. Van Dyne, Linn & Ang, Soon & Ng, Kok & Rockstuhl, Thomas & Tan, Mei Ling & Koh, Christine. "Sub-Dimensions of the Four Factor Model of Cultural

Intelligence: Expanding the Conceptualization and Measurement of Cultural Intelligence." *Social and Personality Psychology Compass.* 6. 10.1111/j.1751-9004 .2012.00429.x. 2012.

4. Kruger J, Dunning D. "Unskilled and Unaware of it: How Difficulties in Recognizing One's Own Incompetence Lead to Inflated Self-assessments." *J Pers Soc Psychol.* 1999; 77(6):1121–1134.

5. Osland, Joyce & Bird, Allan. "Beyond sophisticated stereotyping: Cultural sensemaking in context." *Academy of Management Executive.* 14. 10.5465/ AME.2000.2909840. 2000.

6. Hofstede, G. 1994. In U. Kim, H. S. Triandis, C. Kgitcibasi, S. Choi & G. Yoon (Eds.), *Individualism and collectivism.* Thousand Oaks, CA: Sage, xi.

7. Freire, Paulo, Myra Bergman Ramos, Donaldo P. Macedo, and Ira Shor. *Pedagogy of the Oppressed.* New York: Bloomsbury Academic, 2020.

8. Kumar, Avinash. "Paulo Freire's Pedagogy of the Oppressed: Book Summary," *The Educationist.* July 9, 2014. https://www.theeducationist.info/paulo-freires -pedagogy-oppressed-book-summary/.

Chapter 13

1. Edwards B, Foley MW. Civil Society and Social Capital Beyond Putnam. *American Behavioral Scientist.* 1998; 42(1):124–139.

2. Putnam, R. D. *Bowling Alone. The Collapse and Revival of American Community,* New York: Simon & Schuster, 2000.

3. Fritz, Robert. *The Path of Least Resistance: Learning to Become the Creative Force in Your Own Life.* Kent: Elsevier Science, 2014.

4. Coleman, J. S.. "Social Capital in the Creation of Human Capital." *American Journal of Sociology,* 94, S95, 1988.

5. Edwards and Foley, p. 129

6. Bourdieu, P. "The Forms of Capital." Pp. 241–58 in *Handbook of theory and research for the sociology of education,* edited by J. G. Richardson. New York: Greenwood Press, 1986.

7. Functions of social capital–bonding, bridging, linking, T Claridge—Social Capital Research, 2018

8. Putnam, Robert D. *Bowling Alone: The Collapse and Revival of American Community.* New York: Simon & Schuster, 2000.

9. Stone, Wendy and Jody Hughes. *Social Capital: Empirical Meaning and Measurement Validity.* Australian Institute of Family Studies, 2002.

10. "The Social Capital of Structural Holes," In 2002 *Russell Sage Foundation book, New Directions in Economic Sociology*, edited by Mauro F. Guillen, Randall Collins, Paula England, and Marshall Meyer

11. Healy, Tom, Sylvain Côté, John F. Helliwell, and Simon Field. *The Well-Being of Nations: The Role of Human and Social Capital*. Paris: Organisation for Economic Co-operation and Development, 2001.

12. Rogers, Everett. *Diffusion of Innovations*, 5th Edition. Simon and Schuster, 2003.

13. Rogers, *Diffusion of Innovations*.

14. Diamond, J. *Guns, Germs, and Steel: The Fates of Human Societies*. W.W. Norton & Company.

15. Rogers, *Diffusion of Innovations*.

Index

About the Author

For more than 20 years, Amri Johnson has been instrumental in helping organizations and their people create extraordinary business outcomes. He is a social capitalist, epidemiologist, entrepreneur, executive coach, and inclusion strategist. Amri's dialogic approach to engaging all people as leaders and change agents (previously at the research division of Novartis, as Global Head of Cultural Intelligence and Inclusion) has fostered the opening of minds and deepening of skill sets with organizational leaders and citizens, enabling them to thrive and optimally contribute to one another and their respective organizations.

With an English and biology degree from Morehouse College and a Master's degree in Public Health from Emory, currently Johnson is CEO/ Founder of Inclusion Wins building a global cooperative of people-focused solution providers whose work is informed and enhanced by inclusiveness. His mission is to inspire thousands of organizations around the world to thrive via inclusive behaviors, leadership, structures, and practices. And, for organizational leadership to choose humanity in all decisions they make.

Born in Topeka, Kansas (USA), Amri has worked and lived in the U.S., Brazil, and currently lives in Basel, Switzerland, with his wife Martina and their three kids.